Also by Abigail B. Calkin

Nonfiction:

Pebbles, Mops, and Thimigs (1974)

Eating with a Spoon (1975)

Toilet Training: Help for the Delayed Learner (1978)

Performance Enhancement Training: Change Your Thoughts, Feelings, & Urges (2009)

The Night Orion Fell (2012)

Fiction:

Nikolin (1994)

The Carolyne Letters (1995/2013)

THE *Soul*
OF MY
Soldier

Praise for *The Soul of My Soldier*

"Abigail Calkin's memoir is a beautifully written, deeply honest, and necessary book. This memoir blew me away."

—ABIGAIL THOMAS, author of *A Three Dog Life* and *Safekeeping*

"Calkin gives a unique and very personal account of what it is like, from a wife's perspective, to live with a career soldier and veteran of three combat tours in two very different wars. Abigail Calkin recounts the issues faced and the coping skills acquired over a decades-long marriage. Her stories and descriptions are at once instructive and yet deeply touching in the unfolding. She takes the time to give her biography so we might understand where she is coming from in the relationship.

I served briefly in Vietnam as a young aviator, but have seen the wounds, physical and otherwise, that war inflicted on many returning veterans. Much later, I served as the Senior Director for Gulf War Illnesses on the National Security Council with responsibility for policy direction to improve DoD's response to the veterans returning from that war. No two wars are the same, yet the physical and mental anguish sustained in every one of them have remarkable similarities. Since the Vietnam War, our nation's armed forces have made great strides in recognizing the effects of PTSD, yet still we have not found effective ways to ensure all returning veterans find care sufficient to create coping skills to counter its effects, especially after separation from the Service. Abigail's book offers an insider's view of how one person has managed. More importantly, she gives us a personal perspective of what a soldier's family, and especially the spouse, encounters in the relationship. This is a very different viewpoint than that normally encountered in reading about PTSD and one that has long been needed."

—PAUL BUSICK, Rear Admiral, USCG(ret.)

"Calkin delves deeply, recounting the last 50+ years of her personal life, including her own struggles with trauma, and how she has coped with her lingering symptoms. Uniquely, she intersperses poetry throughout the work, which adds dimension and intensity to her revelations of life as the spouse of a soldier. Masterfully, Calkin outlines her culturally rich American roots, depicting herself as a feisty, yet sensitive woman; and a brilliant professional. Her appreciation for the sacrifices of American service members appears as primal and tangible as her respectful adoration of her husband, an Army veteran. . . . Calkin's description of her own marriage appears to be a metaphor for military service itself, whereby persistence and commitment to something larger than oneself delivers intrinsic rewards in spades."

—KENT A. CORSO, PsyD, OEF Veteran and President of NCR Behavioral Health

"Calkin deftly moves between prose and poetry in this affecting memoir of marriage. Ghosts of hard experiences weave through her words to reveal the power unresolved trauma wields on a relationship. Ms. Calkin reflects themes common to us all by lifting her emotional stones to expose what lies beneath."

—NANCY HUGHES, PhD, LSCSW

"When the guns fall silent and troops return home, soldiers carry with them an emotional mine field. Through intimate poetry and honest prose, Calkin ventures into this treacherous terrain with courage. *The Soul of My Soldier* reveals the tender attentiveness required to survive and heal."

—HANK LENTFER, author of *Faith of Cranes*

"This is a powerful and poignant memoir. Right from the beginning, Calkin acknowledges that she will never understand what her spouse or other soldiers have gone through and she openly admits that this book is about her 'quandary.' The stories and poems are one woman's honest depiction of the challenges she has negotiated with her partner over the years. Her insights about PTSD and her sense of humor and compassion facilitate healing and learning. Calkin's desire to document her story may well offer those who have friends and family in the military the assurance that they are not alone. Above all, this book is a testimony of the love she has for Robert."

—DEE HORNE, Editor of *Scroll in Space*

THE *Soul*
OF MY
Soldier

Reflections
of a
Military Wife

ABIGAIL B. CALKIN

Published by Familius LLC, www.familius.com

Familius books are available at special discounts for bulk purchases for sales promotions or for family or corporate use. Special editions, including personalized covers, excerpts of existing books, or books with corporate logos, can be created in large quantities for special needs. For more information, contact Premium Sales at 801-552-7298 or email specialmarkets@familius.com.

Some of the poetry and prose in *The Soul of My Soldier* have been previously published in *Scroll in Space, Poetry Repairs, Inscape,* and *Reflections.* Thanks to Ed Mercer for his poem, "Home Front," published in the *Topeka Capital-Journal.* Thanks to Theresa Hammett Steinlage for use of her poem, "Response," published in *Poetry Repairs.*

Library of Congress Catalog-in-Publication Data
2015940071

Paperback ISBN 9781942672944
E-book ISBN 9781942934189
Hardcover ISBN 9781942934196

Printed in the United States of America

Edited by Michele Robbins
Cover design by David Miles
Book design by Brooke Jorden

10 9 8 7 6 5 4 3 2 1

First Edition

To

Robert, the man I love

To

the people who serve
and those who live with them

To

the families and buddies of those
who did not come home

Few things are as painful as an invisible wound.

Nelson Mandela

Disclaimer

Whose soul? His, mine, that of the relationship, or is *The Soul of My Soldier* a metaphor for the soul of any soldier?

When I showed my husband the publisher's proposed draft of the book cover, he was shocked. "I don't want anybody to see my soul," he said. "This is a book of fiction, right? You're not talking about me. You don't mention my name, right? I want you to put my disclaimer in there."

I was blindsided. Evidently he was, too. Suddenly, he acted as if I had never mentioned the book, we had never talked about it, and this was his first knowledge of it. Since then, he has teased or somberly reminded me about snippets of previous comments he's made.

What a quandary. I wrote this to honor my husband and be true to myself. I wrote these pieces because I realized that I have my own issues concerning what sometimes seemed to me to be a surprise marriage to my soldier and the military. If I had married someone who had never been in the military, I probably would not have given many stray thoughts to those who serve or to their families. I don't think I honor him by hiding from, denying, or ignoring his service. It is embedded in our lives and has been since the evening we met.

Perhaps I should honor that there are many issues he hasn't confronted and just scrap the whole thing. Perhaps I should break my signed contract with the publisher. But even Robert would say, no, you made a commitment, and you should follow through. Or, as he hollered out the pickup window when driving to another part of the property, "Post humus!" There was that humor and gorgeous smile that so often light up his face and eyes.

"I am confronted by whose story this is." A young husband said of his wife's return, he couldn't talk about her story because it was hers, and he was not a part of it. Having been married for over forty years, I disagree. It has long been undeniable that it has become my story, too.

Had he read the manuscript, I would have taken out anything he requested. I placed individual parts on the table. I told him certain things would go in the book. I placed the entire manuscript on the dining room table. "This is the story I'm telling. This is what I've written. Please read it."

"No," he kindly replied, "put it away. I'm not going to read it. I know you like to write, you know I support your writing, but I'm not going to read it." I had to move forward without his input but with what I felt was his approval.

I have done my best to honor my husband and every other soldier and spouse by writing this and saying things that no one else seems to have said. I think I have also honored myself by writing the truth as I see it. I have kept these thoughts private for over half my life. When I mention the book to others, they immediately respond with war stories from their families—an anecdotal reaction that surprises me every time.

Do I honor my husband? Yes, indeed, but I also need to honor his service and the impact it has had on our marriage and life together. So it is with the kindest and deepest respect to my husband and to every other military marriage that I offer this disclaimer.

Contents

III. Robert and Abigail | 85

IV. Deployment | 109

V. Listen, America! | 143

VI. Recovery | 155

VII. Resolution, Always Partial | 175

Welcome Home | 207

Introduction

*T*his book is a love story about two people and the family they created. Caught in the events of history, like thousands of others across millennia, we had no part in creating the war but bore a miniscule portion in its resolution. This could be a story of any military family in any country. The soldier's iliad goes beyond himself when he leaves a family at home. It is not just he who changed and possibly is recognizable only to the family dog, but the family changed as well. Children have grown. The wife or husband has become more independent or more emotional. War, like any profound experience, changes us.

Before my husband, Robert, deployed to the Gulf War, I became chair of his unit's family support group. I felt the power of being married to a man about to deploy again. I was very much the wife of a soldier. When he came home six months later, I lost that feeling. Years later, while sitting at my desk one autumn day, I realized for the second time in forty years that I was the wife of, no, *am* the wife of a soldier, who was both enlisted and an officer. I now realize that this reality will never change.

I started to write this book when Donna Lee, the wife of poet Li-Young Lee, asked me about the camel pendant I wear. As the writing progressed, I learned and understood more about my husband, more about what is normal when married to someone who's been to war. After reading twenty or thirty books written by soldiers or marines and a memoir by a military wife, and after writing these stories, I learned I will never fully understand. What I read opened my eyes and gave me greater appreciation and respect for my husband and some of his actions, but I cannot comprehend what he lived through. Not all of these writings focus on him. At least half come from stories I've heard or from other people I have met. This book is about my quandary when I think about people going to war. I just happen to be married to one of those who went, which makes me acutely aware of the consequences for individuals and their families.

In addition, these reflections are the odyssey of my emotions and reactions to what I have seen and still see and experience because I am the wife of a soldier, even when a particular story is not about either of us. Our marriage is, as I recently told a friend, a well-negotiated relationship. That process took years. All relationships involve some negotiations, military ones, I think, more than others. I had to set aside my emotions and opinions to observe whom I married and find the most comfortable way to live with the man I love. I know he has done the same. He tells people he has learned to say, "Yes, dear" to statements that used to precipitate arguments. I have learned to stop or take a left turn at the light that signals an argument is coming.

Robert read my first novel, *Nikolin*. He also read large portions of my nonfiction book about a commercial fishing accident, *The Night Orion Fell*, and offered excellent suggestions, but this one? No, he could not read it. A fellow writer suggested I not include a particular piece unless I showed it to him. I thought long and hard. I wonder if I have outed him (or outed me). What does he think of what I've written? I asked him three times to read the manuscript, and each time he declined. I asked him to read individual pieces. For the most part, he declined that also. He read my poem "Comforting the Remnants of My Soldier." I assured him before and after he read it that it came from an interview I heard on the BBC. The soldier had been badly wounded. As my husband read the four-line poem, his facial expression changed from normal to depressed. I said again, "It's not about you," to which he replied he knew that, but he'd seen too many soldiers like the one this poem is about. He read "Why He Is Who He Is" and said that one made him feel sad. Three times he has brought up the book, volunteering that I should pursue it. Although some military and nonmilitary people have read more of it than he has, I, of course, greatly value his opinion. I wonder if I should listen to his words or look at his actions. The answer is not easy. I know him well enough that when he takes a strong stand for or against something, he's firm in action and statement. This time he is not, and that left the decision up to me.

Both of us are shy about publishing. Robert is shy because he likes to blend into a crowd. I am shy about being public with such personal information. Novels and other nonfiction are easy for me, but this nonfiction is about me, and includes my anger, sadness, and other not-so-pleasant parts. This book contains stories of our married life and also the emotional architecture of our marriage. It reveals the blueprint and bricks of a connection that is real but invisible. It shows aspects of our emotional lives which we have woven together. No matter how long we've been married, my descriptions of events and feelings are not his; he holds the more accurate version of his life. My recollections and interpretations of his words and actions are woven into my role as his wife and partner. If he were to read this, I'm sure he'd have corrections about facts, but since he won't, I have to rely on my memory and interpretation of his words and reactions.

Who am I? Who is he? How did we build this life together? How do we negotiate the boggy swamps of disagreement? Every argument, even after forty-four years of marriage, feels like the one that will cause the foundation to crumble. Still, we stand together. I think the credit for that is mostly his. His kindness and sense of humor take a situation fraught with peril and change it into something practical, funny, and tender. He is a man I respect, admire, appreciate, and love.

Abigail B. Calkin

1 January 2015, Alaska

On a practical note, I have done two things. I use *soldier* most often, as it is a soldier I married. I also use the pronoun *he* when the person may be man or woman because my soldier is a man.

I refer to my husband as *Robbie* or *Robert,* and sometimes by what his rank was at the time. When I met him, he had left the army. When he re-upped, he was a sergeant. He later became a second lieutenant, first lieutenant, captain, and finally Major Giese.

i. Early Years

The Camel

*A*t was June 2009 at an inn on Kachemak Bay, Alaska. Donna, someone I had just met, said, "Tell me about your camel."

My camel? I live in Alaska. She's from Chicago, the wife of a poet, and it's her first trip here. People ask me lots of strange questions. Do you have electricity? Running water? An indoor toilet? My camel—do I also have a camel? There used to be camels in Alaska. Camels, mastodons, tigers, and migrating peoples. I have a 145-pound dog, an Akbash, which people ask about. Do I have a camel, too?

Seeing my confusion, she touched her neck. "The camel. The camel around your neck."

I touched my gold camel. "My husband brought it back to me when he came home from the Gulf War." After the now-usual thank-you for his service, she asked how he was.

Fine. From this one. He was not fine after two years in Vietnam. As I shared a story about him, her eyes brimmed with tears.

In 2004, I decided to wear the camel, another necklace, and the earrings he brought back for me until all are back from Iraq and Afghanistan. It's my daily reminder we have people at war.

The following spring, and ever since, many people have asked about my camel—odd, because no one had asked in the five years before.

I wear my camel because it was a gift from my husband. I wear my camel so I remember and think about those who are at war. I wear my camel as a tribute to those who serve in a war zone.

Meeting

I drove the seventy miles home from work on a hot July day. I felt like going into Eugene to stop by Sandy's house and chat; however, that meant that I would still need to get in my car and drive the thirty miles in the mid-nineties heat. I lived out in the country on the McKenzie Highway. I knew it would be ten degrees cooler there, and I could always put on my bikini and sit in the river to cool off.

As I rounded the turn into the barrow pit that separated my house from the highway, I saw a truckload of cattle and an older man in overalls. *Poor fellow,* I thought. *He came to the Willamette Valley to buy cattle and is now headed back to his meager ranch in eastern Oregon, and he loses a wheel.* I slowed to less than five miles an hour in order not to cover him with dust, parked my car by the house and walked back to see what assistance he might need.

He had nothing to do with the cattle. He worked for Fish and Game and was following a pickup with a large trailer loaded with cattle. Weaving badly, it was obviously in trouble. He slowed so he could keep an eye on it. It was not much later a wheel came off the trailer, flew across the road, hit an oncoming loaded log truck on the bumper, and ricocheted off, flying over the pickup, its trailer, and the Douglas firs alongside the road and barrow pit. Relieved he had not caused the log truck to swerve, the pickup driver pulled into the barrow pit, followed by the green Fish and Game pickup as the log truck continued to barrel down the highway to one of the mills.

The cattle driver went to the closest house, mine, to ask to use the phone. With no one there, he tried the next house, my landlord's, with its white fences and four horses pastured there. No answer. He ran up to Greenwood Drive and checked several houses there. No one was home at 5:00 on this Tuesday afternoon. By the time he jogged back to the now very noisy cattle and the barrow pit, I had arrived home and walked back to the trailer and the older man standing there.

What I saw was a young man running along Greenwood Drive, the nearby road that curved about fifty feet above the barrow pit. He ran down the McKenzie Highway and stopped where I stood. I figured he was no younger than sixteen (because he had a driver's license) and probably no older than twenty-one. I was interested. What he saw was a seven-month pregnant woman in a cream-colored dress with vertical stripes of blue flowers. To him, she looked gorgeous because she was attractive and so happy with her pregnancy. To me, he was a drop-dead handsome man with a smile that did not stop. We looked at one another and said nothing.

"You may use my phone."

"Thank you."

The Fish and Game man left, and this young fellow followed me in the house. The owner of the cattle said he'd be up.

The young man and I went out to stand on the deck overlooking the river. We leaned on the railing and began an exchange of conversation that did not stop. He told me he was from eastern Oregon and a Catholic family, but Vietnam took away his religion. He'd come home from two tours in Vietnam, now worked in surgery at McKenzie-Willamette Hospital, and his father was the Lake County sheriff. Surgery was what he'd done in Vietnam, too. I told him I'd never met anyone who'd been to Vietnam, a statement that astonished him and which he'd remind me of a few times some forty years later.

This was 1970 in Eugene, Oregon, one of the nation's hotbeds of war protests. I was oblivious to all this. The evening turned into the longest and most personal conversation I'd ever had with someone who'd been to war. He'd had R&Rs to Bangkok, Japan, and Australia. When he returned home, he found the joint bank account he had with his father empty. This was the account that held all his earnings from Vietnam and the money he was planning to use to move to Australia. His mother was crazy, spent money as if she were wealthy. All his soldier earnings had been spent to try to keep his parents out of debt. His father bought him a red 1969 Rally Sport Camaro with black and white hound's-tooth check cloth seat covers to pay him back. He didn't want it, but what was the option? Now he was saving his money to emigrate.

What did I tell him about myself? I don't remember, but probably that I was a teacher at the college in Monmouth, grew up on the East Coast, went to an Episcopal school and then a Quaker one, lived in Scotland for two years, and would start working at the University of Oregon in the fall. I'm sure we each had various vignettes for one another.

We never talked about the rather obvious pregnancy or where my husband was. All that was irrelevant at the moment.

The doctor who owned the cattle and his friend who owned the brand new trailer arrived before dark. The three of them reloaded the cattle into the trailer. While Dr. Pollard talked to us, he asked my name. What do I tell him? Abigail Koch, I said. I didn't tell him I was married, but my husband had left me four months earlier to move in with someone else. What an idiot he was. About two weeks earlier, I had decided for the first time in my life that I did not need a man to be happy. Why, then, was I changing my last name? I was still unclear on that and a year later decided to stick with the one I'd always had.

Dr. Pollard and his friend left with the cattle as dark approached. A few weeks later, one of his cattle had a calf he named Abigail. He was delighted when he told me that.

The young man and I went back to our conversation on the deck for a couple more hours. When he left, he asked if he could stop by again on his way to his place about twenty miles farther upriver.

"Yes," I said.

The next day he looked in the phone book. All he could remember was

my first name started with an *A* and my last name with a *C* or a *K*. He looked
in the Leaburg/Vida section with all of about two hundred listings. He began
with the *C*s. He was planning to call each one till he found me. He started
with Calkin, A.

I'd been home from work for a while when the phone rang.

"This is Robbie."

Oh my. What a lovely voice on the phone. I stood with my elbows on my
bureau looking into the mirror. I was blushing and my hands shook slightly.
He took some effort to find my number and has called me.

Robbie. How am I going to call a grown man Robbie? If only I'd known
his mother was Irish, I would have called him only Robbie to this day.
Instead, I learned to use it as a term of endearment.

"I'm at my cousin Ernie's goat farm in Harrisburg, and I just wanted to
call you up to tell you I've fallen in love with you."

Fallen in love with me? A deeper red filled my face.

"May I stop by and visit you sometime?"

"Yes."

He stopped by about every two or three days, and we always talked at
length.

After my son was born, he wanted to come by the hospital. Oh my. If
my husband stopped by to see the baby or me—most likely me—I did not
want to have both these men in my room at one time. By this time, I did not
care, but I knew my husband would be lividly jealous. I told Robbie no and
his feelings were hurt. I wondered how I could have complicated my life so
badly.

The doctor and I had planned that I'd stay in the hospital overnight.
However, the birth turned into a cesarean section. The overnight turned into
a week. So much for my plan to save money to take care of my new baby.

Once home, my mother-in-law and Robert's mother became solicitous.
My own mother came from Savannah to help me for a month. I named my
son Seth, and all three of these mothers immediately informed me that Seth
was the third son of Adam and Eve, the one who began all the "begats." ("I

know," I politely responded.) It is also an old Calkin and Burgess family name used every generation since at least the early 1600s.

About a week later, Robbie called me from the eastern Oregon desert to tell me hello and say that he still loved me. He said, "Oh by the way, I hope you're not mad at me, but the day you checked out of the hospital, I went by and paid your hospital bill." A bill of $1,372.00.

What? I thought as I managed to utter a profoundly felt thank you. No one had ever done anything like that for me. This man was definitely turning into someone I would consider as a keeper.

I could figure out later about being a Quaker and, as it turned out, living with a man who'd spent three years in the military. So I thought then. Surely it wouldn't be that difficult to reconcile my attitudes about pacifism and non-violence with the thoughts of a man who had returned from Vietnam with thoughts that we should not be involved in the war there.

When we first met he told me he was planning to move to Australia in December. The move soon turned into a month's vacation there. He has never returned to Australia.

A Drive through Oregon Mountains

*I*n the fall of 1971, with Seth in his car seat, Robert drove our Volkswagen Squareback along dirt roads in the mountains of Oregon's Coastal Range. We both wore Shrink-to-Fit 501 Levis. He had on his green, yellow, white, and black flannel shirt—one I never cared for, but he liked it—and I, a long-sleeved blouse and my favorite sweater, a dark lavender V-neck, one I'd bought when I lived in Scotland as a university student. I'd put our rain jackets in the back seat along with Seth's diaper bag.

I asked a naive question. "Who was the first person you saw dead?" If such a question didn't show my complete lack of manners, common sense, and knowledge of what it meant for him to have been an altar boy serving in the Catholic Church at open casket funerals, working in surgery these days, and an OR tech in a frontline field hospital in Vietnam, nothing did. I received a withering look and no response.

As I write this I am reminded of Lily Burana, author of *I Love a Man in Uniform*, telling of the time she asked her husband how many people he had killed, another question a wife should never ask. I cringed when I read her sentence because, by then, I knew. I understood what must have been her feelings when she heard his remark—even your buddies don't ask you that. Too bad we didn't cringe before we asked our husbands such questions.

In the car that clear fall day, Robert told me a story about a woman walking down a road with a prolapsed uterus, then seeing a dead person on the side of the road. Perhaps that was one and the same person, or the information was so overwhelming to me I got the images mixed up. I tried to picture such a scene but all I came up with were questions: What's a prolapsed uterus? How could you see that if the woman was dressed? Such was the level of my ignorance. At least I had the good grace not to ask him to clarify.

As he continued with stories, tears came. He took his hands off the steering wheel, flailed them in the air to wipe away webs of memory and said, "I don't want to talk about it anymore." With the baby in the back and on these roads, I never asked again . . . for forty years. *How do I read this man?* I wondered. Cautiously. Seriously.

I still wonder that and continue to be drawn in by his straight-faced, practical but kind stories that a leprechaun might tell. He sees common sense and humor in everyday life and talks as if he doesn't possess a dark bone in his body. He is never flippant and has never joked about death or his years in the army. He is a gentle soul, and his life is about taking care of people in medical or psychological need and helping anyone, from family to strangers.

Across the years, he shared a few war incidents with me until he retired from the Army Reserves in 2000, the Iraq war started, and we filled out his retirement paperwork. Then stories came out by the armload. Some were repeated with new details, others stayed the same. Still others were new to me, like driving one of the big trucks from Qui Nhon to Pleiku. Metaphorically, we still drive through the Oregon mountains as he tells more stories. I see his pain in a comment or situation, but I do not comprehend the loneliness he must still feel. I do not always remember the unspoken rules that I sometimes break at the high cost of upsetting him, and I often remain baffled by his vehement response, such as why he brought the car over on the ferry when that means he needs to leave a day early to return to work. "Because I wanted to," or "Because I could bring over more freight." I hope most of the time I remember not to challenge him and his illogical (to me) reasons.

I am glad for the men and women who trained and shipped over together to Iraq and Afghanistan. The units who trained together for Vietnam were not shipped together. The members of the units who were stationed there did not stay with their units if they were needed elsewhere. In his two years,

Robert was in six different MASH hospitals all over the country. He stayed in touch with only two people, and now we don't know where they are. Perhaps if he had stayed with the group he trained with, I would not see his dark side so often, because he'd share it with his buddies. Then again, perhaps I'm very privileged that he shares those thoughts and feelings with me, whether they come out calmly or in turmoil. I know he trusts me.

Forty years later, after listening to the news from Iraq or Afghanistan, Robert made a comment, perhaps about the tragedy of the number killed. I asked a question I knew I'd never ask, but that had haunted me for several years: "How many dead have you seen—four hundred, five hundred?"

"At least," he replied matter-of-factly. The conversation continued, but I don't remember about what—the tragedies of war, our plans for the day, or what we were going to fix for supper. I felt a wave of compassion for this man who has seen so many and accepts it as some level of normal.

Finding the Boundaries

*T*he year after we met, we bought twenty acres of woods outside Eugene, Oregon. We intended to build a cabin and live there. In addition to building a bridge and laying a culvert, we wanted to survey the property lines since our land went from one neighbor's southeast corner to another's southwest corner and on. We carried Robert's new purchase of an antique transit with its wooden box and tripod, his chainsaw, and Seth in the backpack up the steep hill. I leaned the backpack upright against a sizeable fir tree. Robert cut small trees and brush out of the line of sight, and I tossed them aside for clearer walking. He sighted the small, white, metal stake as I positioned it slightly uphill or down to meet the crosshairs. I then drove it into the ground and we continued on to the next. Seth, in toddler boredom, fell asleep in his backpack.

We'd been up there for a while when Robert suggested making love. I couldn't. Nor could I tell him about my primal urge to be on full alert. Work did not distract me from attending to my sleeping child's possible needs, but I knew that making love would. I could move brush or help sight a line because I could listen to or glance at my child. I could not, however, afford to lose myself in my husband's touch. I felt like a she-wolf protecting her cub. What if a coyote came along? A wolf? Or a bear? I protested but could not explain. I stood immobile in front of my sleeping child. Robert shoved me on my shoulder. That was a first. I reacted violently. I pushed this man who weighed fifty pounds more than I hard enough to knock him backward and off balance. He fell and tumbled twenty feet down the hillside into a patch of blackberry brambles. Angry but now in control, neither of us commented, and we continued to survey for the rest of the day.

A few days later, I sat in a chair in the living room reading, and his mother sat staring at nothing. Robert came downstairs yelling about something. I continued to read, aware that his rage had nothing to do with me. When he took the corner to the kitchen, he was too close to the floor lamp and bumped it. Still reading, I reached out to steady it.

His mother rose out of her stupor to declare, "Don't you hit Abigail!"

"Don't worry. I wouldn't dare," he snarled back.

The Summer of 1976

*A*t had been a rough spring. We'd met six years earlier, lived together for the first three, and been married for three. How is it that two people who met by literal and metaphorical accident could look into one another's eyes and in that instant see not only the present beauty but also the history of trauma? The American Psychological Association wouldn't define PTSD for another four years, let alone the country comprehend it till the aughts of the twenty-first century when it became almost a household term as men and women returned from Iraq and Afghanistan.

The summer of 1976 almost turned into Robert's and my waterloo. We had moved to Kansas, so I could go to graduate school. He was a stay-at-home dad, complete with cleaning our married-student housing apartment, doing the grocery shopping, cooking, and carpooling kids to kindergarten. My job was to study and impress the department with my grades. We had very little money. I suffered horrid allergies and a November miscarriage. As I came home from my overnight stay in the hospital, we held hands as we walked slowly from the car up the hill to the apartment, Seth on one side of me, Robert on the other. We told Seth I had lost the baby. He'd already decided it was going to be a girl, and he had named her Sarah. I tried to tell him it could be a boy, but he insisted he would have a sister. As for his choice of names, how could I tell him I really didn't want a Seth and a Sarah in the same family, because I'd constantly get the names confused? I didn't. I just resigned myself to naming her Sarah if she were a girl. As we walked, Seth said, "That's okay, Mommy. If we decide to have another one, we can try again sometime." Obviously, this was a family project.

Robert started university second semester as a freshman. Not having had any intention of ever going to college, he panicked. We argued our way through probably just about everything, hopefully not in front of our son. Things came to a head when Seth's grandparents arrived to take him to Oregon for the summer.

One day as we argued, Robert made not the best of statements. "This is ninety percent your fault!"

I can still hear my childish voice as I yelled a whine back, "No, it's not. It's fifty-fifty." As I heard my words, I thought, *He's right. It is ninety percent my fault.* But I wasn't going to admit it. At least not that decade.

I said one time too many that this marriage wasn't working, and he needed to move out. Be careful what you wish for: you may get it. We drove to a rural area of Kansas, bought a piece of lake property we couldn't afford, and on the way back to Lawrence went to Kansas City for lunch at Crown Center. We entered the parking garage, and he drove through the levels of ace of spades, hearts, diamonds, clubs, on down through the kings, queens, jacks, and tens until we arrived at the ten of clubs. I couldn't figure out why he parked where he did. We had long ago passed floors of empty parking places. We made love in the car on the ten of clubs level, probably the first time either of us had done that in a car. We giggled, went for lunch, drove home, and he moved out. At least that's my recollection.

I was a wreck some days, closing all the curtains and refusing to leave the apartment or answer the phone. Who cared? No one, evidently. It was during a university break, and everyone pretty much left me alone.

A week after he'd moved out, he called me. Expecting an argument, I felt tension build in my throat, but he called to ask me out for a date. A date. No one had asked me out for a date for . . . I don't know, it felt like not since I was a teenager. With a skip in my heart and a smile on my face, I accepted. I don't know where we went or what we did. I just remember treating it like a date with someone I didn't know all that well. Maybe that was his purpose— let's get rid of the history and investigate a relationship. I remember walking across campus with him, hoping he would reach out and hold my hand. I don't know whether he did. I remember only the hope. He suggested going to his place.

"Sure," I answered with some apprehension. What was going to happen? What did he have on his mind? I liked him a lot. I agreed to go. I'd always been a bit of a risk taker. This afternoon had taken on all the elements of a date and none of our troubled marriage.

It was a one-room apartment with a desk and chair, a double bed, and two upholstered chairs. I sat in one, he in the other. It seemed like they were fifty feet apart, a safe distance. He asked me if I was in a relationship, involved with or seeing anyone. I said I was but we were having problems. I described the situation (did I say "marriage"?) to him as if he were a stranger. What I learned from the telling enlightened me as he listened and said nothing. When I finished my tale of a relationship in trouble, I asked him the same question and listened while he responded. I *listened*. I heard. I learned. I saw the mistakes I was making. I saw I was breaking his heart, just as he was breaking mine. After slipping back and forth between this date, discussing our marriage as if to a different person, and probably making love in his bed, he walked me home then returned to his place for the night.

We'd gone for marriage therapy before. The first time, we took charted data of our feelings and interactions. The therapist was very interested in what we showed and told him, but said he had nothing to offer; we had analyzed beyond his level. Next time we found a highly recommended couple. After one meeting then months of delay because one or the other of them was out of town, we met with them to hear that they had certain rules about how we should conduct our marriage. We had already stated how we wanted our marriage to be when we first met with them. Now, here they were four months later, telling us we had to change the structure of what we wanted. We got up and walked out. We then went to the University of Kansas Psychology Clinic and made an appointment. Just as a renter or a landlord can turn down a rental, we stated to some poor advanced graduate student therapist that we were not taking another personality test, asked what his rules and approach were, and explained what our rules and needs were. At least Robert and I agreed on something. Could he work with us? He said yes, and he was right. We worked with this man for perhaps a year.

I went back to him, then another therapist occasionally, for about ten years. Yes, Robert was right. It was 90 percent me. Two people in one marriage, each with their own varying and periodic levels of PTSD, makes for what someone once told us was "a good Italian marriage." We knew how to scream and yell, and we knew how to make things right in the bedroom afterward.

What kept us together? Tolerance. Loyalty. We are both youngest children who remain willing to say the other might be right. Love. Laughter. Kindness. Not running away from issues. Robert's perpetual honesty. My determination to mend—to mend me. A perpetual desire to work hard all the time. What's that line from *The Hurt Locker*, a movie about the soldier who disarmed IEDs? Something about needing the adrenaline fix.

The need for the fix comes, and its purpose is to be noisier than the dragons of the problem. When the person doesn't address the dragons though, the habit begins to maintain on its own. Robert's and my dragons roamed for so long, we were each left with a habit of working hard all the time. We felt we were loafing if we took a vacation or even a day off.

He moved back in before Seth came home at summer's end. We met his plane together in Kansas City. He was the last one off and in the arms of a flight attendant. We sent him off as the son of two college students, but he returned home a western kid—long-sleeved snap shirt, jeans, a ten-gallon hat, cowboy boots, short haircut, and a box with his holsters and six-shooters. Robert and I watched and wondered if this was our son. He was the right age, but looked very different from the boy we sent away. The little boy began to wave. We looked around and saw there was no one but us. We waved tentatively. As they came closer we recognized his beam of a smile. We settled into our life as a family, Robert and I still struggling as individuals and a couple for the next ten years before we settled into our own lives and a much calmer relationship.

When Seth was twenty-one, he called me from Oregon or Alaska.

"You know that Italian family?" he asked redundantly.

"Yes. You never really were a part of it, were you?"

"No."

Later in the conversation, he said, "Mom, I love you very much, but I don't want to marry a woman like you."

I smiled then; I smile now. With a grateful sigh, I thought, *What a good job we did of raising this young man who did not bend under our issues, but maintained the integrity of his calm, quiet demeanor.*

PTSD

PTSD stands for post-traumatic stress disorder. The stress may occur from one incident so powerful it overwhelms a person, or it may occur from multiple incidents. Being raped, assaulted with a deadly weapon, or held hostage are some situations that may affect a civilian. Dare I say, never having been in a war zone, that watching people die or holding a dying buddy who covered your back may be ones that stand out in war?

I could rattle off any of my situations that plunked me in the PTSD category, but I spare the details. I usually don't even say that much. Some of those details are in other books I've written. Suffice it to say here that they are traumas that unwittingly keep coming back as flashbacks.

Decades ago a friend, whose husband had been killed in Vietnam, and I sat in a restaurant eating supper and drinking too much as we compared histories. We listed our various crises, and wondered how we survived to be successful without going over the precipice. Some people we worked with had had fewer severe crises and not survived as intact as we had. I've looked at mine, turned them over and over, examined them as if with the microscopic eye of a research scientist, crawled out of that muck by hard work, and dissolved them piece by particle. Bad memories no longer arrive unbidden. They rarely come back at all unless I choose to think about them, but I also can now brush them off like lint on the shoulder of a black jacket. I can talk about them without tears or stomach aches or anger or shaking. Yes, there are those very occasional moments when my reactions are excessive or inappropriate, but that's the remnant of a behavior pattern and no longer fear or lack of good options. I have great empathy for those with the unbidden frightening and painful flashbacks, be they girls who've been raped or soldiers who've been to war.

Fifteen years after Robert and I met, I wondered whether some unspoken recognition of one another's unresolved issues gave us a common ground of understanding that first evening. As the years went by, I tolerated his yelling because I yelled back, and the reverse was true. And laugh—oh my—ten minutes after an argument, there he was back with something good for laughter.

What made me mend? I come from good roots with a strong, supportive family—both the one I had when young and the one Robert and I developed. That was not enough though. I had a stubborn determined drive not to stay where I was—stuck in the middle of John Bunyan's Slough of Despair in his *Pilgrim's Progress*, a book I slogged my way through as a child because it spoke to me. No, I was not going to stay stuck in pain.

I was sick of dealing with it, and in 1977, realizing my marriage was once again at stake, I accidentally fell into a way to change it. Every day, I counted the positive and negative thoughts I had about myself and my personal pleasant and unpleasant feelings. I got mad at myself because they were not changing. I finally tried the daily one-minute timing that I did with children when teaching them to read and do math facts. This technique comes from precision teaching, which is a methodology of using a standard chart to measure learning, whether that learning is in an elementary school, nursing, social work, business, or other areas. For the children I changed the material they worked on to easier or harder pages, or rewarded them for learning using a smile and comment or a positive phone call the two of us made to a parent. I hoped if it worked for children, it would work for me.

As it turned out, this technique I developed began a new line of research about thoughts, feelings, and urges into the field of behavior analysis. I timed myself for one minute every day. During this minute I wrote all the positive things about me that I thought or felt. I made a master list of these positives and have added to that since. When a negative thought or feeling occurred,

I counted backward from ten to one, slid into a relaxing imaginary place—down a water slide into a Kansas farm pond, and floated as I flooded myself with my positives. I tried to change that image. First, I didn't swim well and was terrified of water. Second, and perhaps even more of a problem, sliding into that pond is so disgusting it's laughable. A Kansas farm pond is full of piss and manure from cattle . . . but the image wouldn't go away. I had to decide my pond was clean and blue . . . or if still brown, at least germ-free.

What amazed me was that I became a calmer person. I began to learn, at least most of the time, when I was responsible for something or when someone else held that responsibility. I watched the negative parts float away from me. I felt my good parts solidify into the whole I knew I could be. I stopped apologizing and started saying thank you when complimented. Discounting compliments—that *Yes, but if you knew the real me* feeling, or *This yellow dress. Heavens, I've had it for years*—began to evaporate.

Oh yeah, I still have a few flashbacks—if not in thought, at least in behavior. Just an old pattern, I acknowledge. My most recent example came a year ago when I put gas in Seth's newest diesel work truck. I could not calm myself and could not think clearly. It took my five-year-old granddaughter and my daughter-in-law to calm me down from my hysterical reaction. The next morning, I realized how muddled my thinking had been that afternoon.

In one of my recent conversations with my friend, Susan Farmer, a poet and psychiatrist, I said I thought I probably had PTSD worse than Robert did. In her very calm and quiet manner, a manner more Quaker than I possess, she said, "I was not going to tell you that." Even over the phone, I heard her smile as I laughed.

Dream on
6 September 2001

*D*epression means what it says: a depressed level of activity. The best frequency information the behavior analysis field has on depression is the following personal, frequency-based description of depression, which occurred as a result of 11 September 2001.

Background: Thursday morning, 6 September 2001, a friend and I were camped at McBride Glacier in Alaska. We had kayaked up from the beginning of the East Arm for a week of camping and paddling. With two days left in the trip, I awoke from a dream in which two planes crashed into some objects. First one, then the other. A ball of fire emerged from each object and in between flew a helicopter. First one object imploded, then the other. When I awoke that Thursday morning, I spent the next hour writing down all the details of my dream.

As my neighbor and I went on our usual morning walk that Tuesday, 11 September, about 8:00 Alaska time, I learned of the World Trade Center attack. We turned around and went to her house to watch TV. I sat there continually saying, "That's what I saw in my dream. I dreamed that! I saw the helicopter. I saw those implosions." After twenty minutes, I couldn't stand to watch anymore. After all, I'd already seen the whole scene. I walked home.

Wednesday, 12 September, I heard on the 8:00 news that Manhattan was closed from 14th Street on down. I said to my husband, "That's where I *lived*. I went to school there, church, Quaker meeting. I played with my friends, hung out with them in Washington Square." From a sitting position, I immediately lay down and went to sleep till Friday morning. I posted the following to the Standard Celeration List on the Internet, and it was later quoted by two top researchers in bereavement within the field of behavior analysis:

> In my article, "Changes in Behavior as the Result of the Death of a Relative" (Calkin, 1990), I mentioned the depression of behavior & presented three charts of people to show this. What each of the charts shows is a gap in the counting. I have always wanted to have some counts during the depression. I've never been able to get anyone, including myself, to count during a depressed episode— although one of the charts in that article probably does show this. I do know, and now accept, that when a relative or friend learns s/he is terminally ill or when someone close to me dies, my level of activity is depressed for about a month afterwards. Then the healing can begin.
>
> Friday morning, 14 September, I decided to count my behaviors, every one of them. Get teacup, pour milk in it, pour tea in it. Sit. Stand up. Get pillow off chair. Put pillow on sofa. Lie down. Pull blanket over me. Sit up. &c. Pretty basic things. I counted for five hours & in that time did 38 actions. Frequency = .12—just over one action every ten minutes. I did not write one word, although I sat prepared to do that.
>
> Feeling significantly better, on Tuesday, 9 October (four weeks later, I now realize), I felt able to count my actions once again. I knew there would be many so I decided to count for only one hour—the joy of frequency to compare five-hour to one-hour counts. 820 actions. Frequency = 13.5. If I had written one word on 14 September, I'd have counted it as one; thus, I had to count words written this day.
>
> People in my small community were quite concerned about me. As I began to function again this week, they saw me out & about, and asked me (as opposed to asking family, friends & neighbors) how I was doing. I was able to tell them, "I am doing 135 times better."

September 11, 2001

Response

Abigail B. Calkin

As the sun shimmers
Waves wash the brine from our soul
Clouds wrap around us

Fold over purple
mountains, hide the sky from us:
An easterly blows.

Our soul turned inside out
Rinsed in salt
We hold out hands to friends
Invisible before this day.

We stand at Union Square
Chinatown, City Hall
Fly over to land at JFK, LaGuardia,
Smell the stone dust bone
Asphalt wire rebar
That dirt metal and death odor
Seeps into our nostrils,
Tongue, teeth, skin.

As the sun shimmers
Waves wash the brine from our soul
Clouds wrap around us

Fold over purple
mountains, hide the sky from us:
An easterly blows.

Response

Theresa Hammett Steinlage

Ishmael!
Mt. Sinai is constant.
Christ knew.
After him Mohamed, the Ishmaelite knew.
Thou shalt not kill!
You came before. Your mother
Hagar the Egyptian was scorned.
Bore you for Abram –
Her reward the desert dust –
Abandoned son
You screamed your infant's rage until
Angels wept.
Ishmael!
Where is an angel?
We are no sons of Hagar.
Nor daughters – cloistered – disguised – despised.
Penance paid?
Redemption gained?
Ishmael!
You are the child of Abram too.
Hagar's milk is bitter.
Sands sting
Traveling on a western wind
We all burn.
Your children too.
Ishmael, there is no desert.
It is an ocean filled with the bitter milk of
Tears.

Ancestors

I was born in Boston and grew up in Framingham Centre, one of its suburbs. A trip to Boston was always special, not only because I started my life there, but because my mother never took all of us there together. It was a guaranteed day of only my mother and me. No siblings, no aunts or cousins, no father, just the two of us. I know she did that with the others, but I don't remember them being gone. No, Boston with my mother was my day—the Common, Copley Square, Newbury Street, Filene's Basement (the prototype for all the country's discount stores), and Winter and Summer Streets right next to one another. A swan boat ride in Boston Public Garden, walking through the Common, seeing the state capitol building, going into Saint Paul's Church where she and my father were married, going next door to Prey's Oriental Rug Store to browse. Sometimes we also went to the Museum of Fine Arts or to Mrs. Gardener's House. The pièce de résistance, the sine qua non, however was the last stop: Brigham's Ice Cream Shop for the best sundae in the world served in a metal dish with the hot chocolate sauce running over the sides onto the metal plate beneath. She smiled a lot on those trips and seemed less serious. I did my best to be well behaved.

On other days, Peggy Wood, one month younger than I and my best friend since before either of us remember, got together often. Our very older brothers used to take us for walks in our baby carriages, my brother stating with pride, "My sister has curly hair." We climbed the O.A.T.—the Old Apple Tree. We took picnic lunches to the cemetery far enough away for a long bike ride and ate lunch on the flat tombstones under trees that were still cool on a hot summer day. We walked to the Centre, crossing the four-lane Route 9 to go to the library or The Living Room Library, a gift shop where my aunt, who lived with us, worked.

Peggy's mother drove us down the hill till we were old enough, four or five, to ride our bicycles down the hill the other direction to Maple Street, turn right, cross the railroad tracks, and ride on to Hopkinton Road to watch the marathon runners on their way from Hopkinton to Copley Square. There weren't as many then and sometimes we waited a long time before one came by. We heartily cheered them on.

One Boston Marathon day many years later—5 April 2013—someone planted two bombs at the finish line, injuring many and killing some. What was their point?

How can we forget that the American Revolution started here before it spread across the land? In Boston in 1773, people climbed aboard boats docked at the wharf and threw cases of tea overboard. The revolutionary fighting started with the Battles of Lexington and Concord on 19 April 1775. Two months later came the Battle of Bunker Hill, a gently sloping hill no bigger than the Leningrad one where the Russians held off the Germans for nine hundred days on their exposed southwest flank.

I know my ancestors. I grew up hearing their names as if I might meet them some day. Other times it felt as if one of them had walked into a room in our house. As soon as I could, I read four hundred years of tables of generations—names, birth and death dates—with repeated names such as Abigail, Hannah, Mary, John, Seth, Hugh. I read letters and Pennsylvania land deeds from the 1700s. Some sailed the seas while others founded this country. I have been in their homes, walked the streets where they walked, have photographs or paintings of some. I come from a family that fought in war and made munitions for the American Revolution. As I review this history now with a new eye, I can see why I married a soldier.

I went to Joel Ferrée's in Paradise, Pennsylvania. He was a gunsmith who owned a general store. He stored his goods deep in his dirt basement. Low below, in the subbasement, well beneath the food, he made guns and bullets for guerilla revolutionaries, the soldiers who dressed in their everyday clothing and blended into the colors of the forests and fields.

Across the Post Road that ran from Lancaster to Philadelphia, lived David and Esther Witmer and their many children. One of their sons, David Witmer, was my great-great-great-grandfather. David married Jane Lightner. Jane's brother, John Adam Lightner, married Joel Ferrée's daughter, Leah Ferrée. Another one of the Witmers married an Eshleman. Thus, these families of the Revolutionary War mingled across a generation or two to form a good portion of my mother's families. By 1800, they also added a few more staunch founders of the country to become my ancestral core, this family whose roots go back to Charlemagne.

Recently, I realized the contradiction that has survived two centuries. My mother's Mennonite ancestry survived within her to make her a quiet person who wore little jewelry and taught her children not to argue. I don't ever remember a flag displayed from the house, but she was a Gray Lady at the Cushing VA Hospital and supportive of my father's efforts to enlist during World War II.

The first David Witmer was a friend of George Washington's. On what we call an R&R today, George would go to Witmer's house for a few days. He rested, they chatted, and George went to the next farm over to buy grains from the Eshlemans. The Ferrées and the Witmers lived on the north side of Pequea Creek, which also ran through Eshleman's place. I try to imagine life in those days 235 years ago. That is a long time ago, but when my mother talked about her grandmother, Hannah Steele Witmer, and going to her funeral at age fourteen, my great-grandmother Hannah Steele comes alive. She was born in 1809 and lived to be a week shy of 104. She wore a lawn cap in her dotage as her hair had thinned. My mother had a picture of her framed and on the wall, named my sister after her. She had been a child during the infancy of the country and an adult and mother, perhaps even a grandmother, during the Civil War.

David and Esther's stone house is now an inn. I stayed there one night, not because I knew it was their house, but because it was in the area of part of my ancestral home. The innkeepers had researched the Witmer family and knew more details than I did. We sat in the parlor talking of how the elder David sat in here with George Washington when he, the general leading the rebel soldiers to fight the British army, came to visit. The innkeepers put me in the best room, David and Esther's master bedroom. Above the bed were portraits of them, two of the homeliest people I ever laid eyes on. There was nothing appealing in their features. I lay in bed that night thinking my great-great-great grandfather, David Witmer, was conceived in this room. Portions of my beginnings lie here.

On the other side of the family, an ancestor came on the *Mayflower*, and the rest arrived ten and twenty years later. By the first half of the eighteenth century, they had all moved to Nova Scotia. They were more peaceable and some of them became seafarers. Only one went to war. He died in World War I. Two of the seafarers died in the widow-and-orphan-making North Atlantic. Although my father may have been the Quaker, I think he was only the second one who had any interest in joining the military. Why did he try to enlist? Because someone had attacked his country.

Philip Philip Barry

*J*uniper roots become dry and limbs desiccated and twisted, but the stubby trees still grow needles and berries at their tops. So too does oral family history change, in this case across one hundred years. After a 1993 family reunion of several generations and over four hundred people, my mother-in-law, Eleanor Barry Giese told my husband and me her version of this story of an Irish village's conflict and resolution. I then had several versions to meld.

Grandmother Barry, Eleanor's mother, told me about her life in New York City because she had lived two blocks from where I spent part of my childhood. We both seemed to relish that we had lived so close in distance yet apart in time. Like few places in this country, fifty years had done little to change the Greenwich Village neighborhood where we lived. When I heard these stories, I saw Robert's family and the history of war and peace within his and my family.

Like many who joined the military, Robert enlisted because his small town offered him little opportunity, and he knew he was not headed to college. He still remembers sitting on Grandfather's knee. I doubt if Grandfather's participation in resistance to the British fostered Robert's desire to join the military, but it would not have discouraged it. To this day, if we watch a film with Irish accents, Robbie understands the dialogue. If the actors have an English accent, he says he can't understand what they're saying. I think such subtle learning is a part of how we learn prejudice. The Irish and the English have been at war for over four hundred years with periodic flaring of hostilities.

In the late nineteenth century in Ireland, the absentee English landlord still owned most of the country's land. Each family either paid rent on their house, or if they owned it, they still needed to pay an annual fee to live in their dwelling. Presumably, this custom in Ireland corresponded to the custom in Scotland, both probably left over from the Middle Ages. Still extant in Scotland in the 1960s, this practice meant that someone could own the house but not the land on which it sat and had to pay a fee to live there.

In the late 1800s, English landlords hired men to go house to house to collect rent fees. Poor even before the potato famine of 1848, a family often had trouble scraping the funds together. If they did not pay, they were immediately turned out of the cottage. Knowing that some families did not have the money, it occasionally happened that young men of the area intimidated the fees collector who, then, did not return for a few days. This gave a family time to gather more money. As the story goes, the collector was robbed on occasion and the money taken to the next house.

Philip Philip Barry, Robert's grandfather, was born in Tureendarby, Newmarket, County Cork on 31 October 1875, the youngest of six children. His father, Philip Kane Barry, had left for America before he was born, leaving the family to exist on village charity. Philip Philip was named for his paternal and maternal grandfathers. Because the same first and last names are so common in Ireland, many acquired nicknames. Robbie's grandfather became known as Phil Ban'n: *ban'n* or *bawn* being Gaelic for "white." Known as Whiteboys—a term of dignity for the secret society of eighteenth-century men who resisted the Crown's taxes—these teenaged young men wore white hats and waylaid the Protestant rent and tithe collectors for the duration of the nineteenth century. To the Irish, the Whiteboys, probable forerunners of the Sinn Fein, were good boys who fought the English on behalf of their people.

In 1890, Philip Barry, age fifteen, and two friends, Jerry Egan and Dave York, waylaid the local collector. They had probably done this many times before one fatal night. In the melee of confrontation, the collector died either from falling off his horse or a blow to his head. All three young men were arrested and taken to jail.

Jerry and Dave pointed to Phil Ban'n. Phil went to prison and Jerry and Dave forcibly left the country, immigrating to America—Jerry to Lake County, Oregon, and Dave to San Francisco. It would be several decades before Phil ever spoke to either man, their betrayal still hot in his heart. During his ten years of imprisonment, a priest who taught him to read and write befriended Phil Ban'n. In those days, prisons did not provide meals. It was a small girl from the village, Bridget Cotter, the daughter of Phillip Cotter, a prominent and well-off villager, who, according to her father's instruction, took Phil Ban'n his dinner bucket each day, beginning at the tender age of five.

In 1897, Queen Victoria celebrated her Diamond Jubilee and pardoned many prisoners. Philip Philip Barry was one. He immigrated to Lake County, Oregon by way of the Panama Canal and California. In 1901, at the age of twenty-six, he landed in San Francisco and met his father, Philip Kane Barry, (who had left for the States before his son was born) for the first time. The two hardly ever spoke, but Philip Kane was known for not talking much to anyone.

Starting off as a sheepherder, Phil Ban'n took some of his pay in sheep and eventually became a Guano Valley and Long Valley sheep rancher. The sheep and cattle wars were going on in eastern Oregon at this time. By now, Phil had enough sheep to start his own ranch. Some cattlemen caught up with and captured him, then tied him to a wagon wheel and left him to die. One of his sheepherders came upon him in the dry open range and untied him.

Another incident involving Grandfather Barry occurred in 1904. He was driving 1,500 of his sheep and had stopped for the night. While he was asleep in his tent, some men came along, blindfolded him, and tied him up. Initially, Phil thought it was one of his brothers or cousins and hollered at them to stop joking around. Before long though, he realized these men had malicious intent. With Phil Ban'n trapped in his tent, the men then set about killing as much of his herd as they could. It seems that *The Oregonian,*

Portland's and all of Oregon's newspaper, got wind of this and published the event. Western Oregon became so outraged that this triggered the quick end of what had become known as Oregon's Sheep and Cattle Wars. Later, Phil Ban'n, like many other ranchers in the area, ranched both sheep and cattle.

All this time, as Phil made his way in America, he waited for Bridget, the same young girl who had brought him his dinner bucket for the ten years he was in prison. Bridget's brother, Joe Cotter, knew of Phil Ban'n's intent of marriage to his sister. Joe gave Bridget, now age seventeen, the fare for the boat to America, enough money to get as far as New York. In order to travel alone, she had to state she was eighteen, the age shown on Ellis Island records. She lived with a family on the north side of West Ninth Street, between Fifth and Sixth Avenues in Greenwich Village, when she first arrived, working as a seamstress for the family who owned the brownstone house. One of Phil Ban'n's brothers, who also lived in Lake County, said, "Phil, you better go get her. She won't wait much longer." Phil Ban'n took the train back East to fetch his bride. They journeyed by train to Oregon, marrying along the way in Washington, DC, in June of 1909.

He and Bridget had twelve children. They lived at the Shirk Place on the ranch in Guano Valley, and also bought a house in town, 134 South H Street, so the children could attend school. The sixth child and fifth girl they named Eleanor. Phil called her Paddy and doted on this feisty and very-much-like-him child.

In 1942, Eleanor Barry Giese, now herself a young bride, her mother Bridget Cotter Barry, her Uncle Pat Cotter, and her sister Elizabeth Barry left Lake County for a train trip to San Francisco. Shaving and looking steadily in the mirror, Phil Ban'n gave his daughter an order before she left.

"Go see Div Yorrk, 'n' tell hi' I sint ye." He handed her a slip of paper with an address.

"Why?" she asked.

"Go see Div Yorrk, 'n' tell hi' I sint ye," Phil Ban'n repeated.

She put the address in her handbag and left for the city.

The four—mother Bridget, Uncle Pat, Eleanor, and Elizabeth—took a taxi to the address. Eleanor, young and slender, wore a green suit with a matching hat and a fur-trimmed coat. She got out and the others waited in the taxi. She went to the door and rang the bell. A good-looking man, about six feet five inches tall, with glasses so thick they magnified his eyes, opened the door. Having no idea of the looks of the man she was to see, knowing only that Dave York owned a lot of apartment buildings in San Francisco, and seeing that this man was too tall for an Irishman, Eleanor said, "I'm looking for Dave York. My father sent me to see him."

He opened the screen door and grabbed Eleanor, knocking her hat to the ground.

"My God! My God! You're Phil Ban'n's daughter!" he cried. Tears streamed down his cheeks as he held the five-foot-four young lady so tightly it hurt her. He didn't let go and hugged her more and more until she was afraid he'd break her ribs.

"Let go! You're hurting me! Please let go," she cried out.

Dave York finally calmed enough to release her and invited her in.

"But my mother and sister and Uncle Pat are in the taxi."

Patrick Cotter! From home! He rushed to the cab to invite them all in and paid the fare.

Together they walked to the door of his house. His wife was a little bit of a thing who wore her hair in a bun. Dave insisted the guests stay for a turkey dinner. He told his wife to go to the store to buy the turkey, and on her return she fixed the celebratory dinner.

Periodically during the afternoon, as the turkey cooked, Dave York, sitting in his armchair, talked and wept, sometimes muttering, "Forgiveness. Forgiveness."

In the late 1940s, Phil Ban'n and his son-in-law, Con Lynch, were shipping their cattle out of Plush, Oregon. Con did some manipulation at the end of the day and managed to get Phil Ban'n to have a whiskey with Jerry Egan that cold autumn afternoon—their only contact since that fateful day the tax collector died.

The family was left to wonder whether it was Phil or Dave or Jerry who caused the fee collector to fall off his horse. I have also often wondered about these three young men—Phil Ban'n, Jerry Egan, and Dave York. Were they revolutionaries like the Whiteboys of earlier years or Sinn Fein, the group that lay on the horizon?

Roddy and the Dog

*I*t was during World War II. We were little—I was four and Roddy three. He was my cousin Anne's son, and his father, SSgt. John E. Rodgers or Johnny, as everyone in the family and his 464th Army Air Corps bombardier group called him, had been killed on 29 May 1944 on his twentieth mission. He was the ball turret gunner, the most dangerous spot on a plane. The story goes that he wrote Anne, his wife, a letter saying he didn't think he'd make it. The plane was shot down over Austria, and the crew bailed out in Yugoslavia. The pilot became a POW at Dulag Luft Oberuesel. Johnny was severely wounded with machine gunfire across his legs. The tail gunner helped him bail out. He died in a German Luftwaffe hospital that same day, having bled to death from his wounds. Both he and Anne were twenty years old.

My mother was the oldest of six. She and my father took in anyone in need—their own mothers when widowed and two of her widowed sisters lived with us, often for years. My mother's college roommate and her son arrived in 1945 when her husband, who was the Consul General to China, returned to help Chiang-Kai-Chek move his government to Formosa. They stayed for a year. My cousin and her son, Anne and Roddy, stayed for only two weeks, but what made their visit wonderful was that, for the first time, I had a relative my age in the house.

My mother, his grandmother (my aunt), and great-grandmother told me to be nice to him because he'd just lost his father. I knew there was something solemn about this visit.

I had to listen to the radio when Churchill or Roosevelt spoke. My mother sat in the red armchair with the ottoman and Hannah curled beside her, Mary on the floor in front of the fireplace. Bill sat on the wooden antique chair and my father in the red leather chair by the radio. The only spot for me was my father's lap, where I curled against his wool herringbone tweed three-piece brown suit. It scratched my young cheek, but I learned to be comfortable because no one was allowed to talk. I don't know where the other relatives listened to the radio, but there was no room for them in the den. The war news never seemed promising.

Even though Churchill and Roosevelt, Thomas Lowell and *Life* magazine filtered war into our lives, Roddy seemed as unaware of world events as I was. We were two little children happy to have a playmate. One day he found a stuffed dog in my sister Mary's room. We argued about who was going to play with it. Roddy found it and held it by the tail. I had the body and it was *my* house. Possession may be nine-tenths of the law, but we had different definitions of possession. We stood in the large, rectangular hallway tugging and pulling. The dog's tail came off. Oh the wails! Ruckus was not allowed. Down from the third floor came a mother or grandmother. Up from the first floor came my mother. We were summarily sent to our rooms. He was in my brother's room and I in mine. I opened the door into the shared closet and then opened the door into his room. He looked lost sitting there on the bed. I told him I was sorry. He was company, he'd lost his father, I was told to be nice to him, and I hadn't been. I invited him to the closet where my brother stored board and card games. We played a game or two. I left the doors open a crack to hear any approaching footsteps. None came.

Why do I remember that? I think because I could not imagine losing my father whose scratchy wool suit coat and vest I snuggled against when I listened to news I did not understand. My heart went out to my playmate. I also remember it because I think Roddy doesn't, and someone needs to remember moments from that pivotal time of his life.

Last week, I talked to Rod for the first time in many decades. He remembers that time in his life—going to his father's grave in Lancaster, Pennsylvania, taking the train to visit us, seeing the brick buildings of the college across the street, and being told not to touch anything as he watched my teenage brother build model airplanes.

Arlington National Cemetery

*L*ast week, I met Rod's son for the first time. His name is also Rod. We met on my first trip to Arlington National Cemetery where Rod the younger has been the chief curator for eleven months. He showed me around as if it were his backyard, but it wasn't a garden tour of forsythia or rhododendron. Instead he pointed out areas and tombstones with the names of generals or privates from this war or that. He knows his history as if this were about our family. Instead, it is the history of our country's battles from the Civil War till now. He told me about his predecessor standing outside looking at the city of Washington when American Airlines flight 77 clipped a few telephone poles on its way to the Pentagon. He took me to the half dozen Arlington graves of those from the thirty-one killed in the August 2011 Afghanistan helicopter crashes. We saw two families sitting by the gravestones of their sons or daughters killed in Iraq or Afghanistan. He said they bring their chairs and sit there all day. I think I might have done the same, but then again I'm not sure I could.

As the curator, Rod can drive or go anywhere in the cemetery. We went to the amphitheater where the president gives the talk on Memorial Day. He took me down below to a chapel of marble, a location for special funerals. He also took me to his office, underground, below which are the apartments where the Tomb Sentinels live. Above ground again, we walked behind the amphitheater, to the Tomb of the Unknown Soldier guarded by these Sentinels day and night. The sentinels who have this duty wear no name on their uniform and sunglasses to remain as anonymous as the unknown dead.

Except for the occasional click of heels when they change the guard, there is no sound. I wonder about the people who lost someone and waited for the return that never came. Did some mother, father, sister, or brother die with the hope that young man would walk up the path some day?

I had not known how close Arlington was to the National Mall. When I left my cousin and the cemetery, I walked across the Potomac, around the Lincoln Memorial to the Vietnam Wall. This memorial is dedicated not only to the 58,000 who died but also to all who served there. They had fenced off the grass in front of the Wall so I could not sit there this time. I stood by some men my age who looked for the names of those lost from their unit. I watched them and, once again, felt so grateful my Robert's name is not there, but I had a sense of his hovering behind and in front of the reflective black granite because he had walked through the intimacies and horrors of death and personal destruction into my arms and life. That evening I called to tell him about the men who came to see their buddies' names. I told him how much I loved him, how grateful I am he ran into my life, how grateful I remain that his name is not on that wall. I told him what an immense difference he has made to Seth and me. He responded softly. I told him I found the three from his hometown—his classmate Paul Sheer, his sister's classmate, Layne Simpson, and Jim Carlson, whose death was personal to my husband. He was touched.

Half a million was a lot of death to view in one day even though I saw no tombs or names I knew. As the evening wore on, my country's stories of war weighed upon my head and shoulders. Depression enveloped me like a green Kansas sky with its black storm clouds creeping in from the southwest. I cried myself to an early sleep knowing I had to be cheerful for work the next two days, especially since I was going to talk about war, its impact on people's lives, and post-traumatic stress disorder.

708

When Robbie was seven, his parents bought a house whose number is 708. Within the family we refer to it that way. It's on a corner and has a huge side yard for an in-town house in a small town in ranch country. It's two-story and white with green shutters and a green roof, good for Irish country. Built in 1933 by someone who owned one of the timber companies, its construction is of good lumber and high-quality craftsmanship. Typical of 1930s design, it has archways from the entryway to the living room and from the living room to the dining room. The fireplace has side vents that help disperse the heat. The kitchen is large and has a breakfast nook at the end of it, again with the arch. The first floor bedroom has two cedar-lined closets and the bathroom another archway to the tub.

His parents bought it in 1957, complete with its furniture, dishes, silverware, and linens. The floral patterned English wall-to-wall carpet was so familiar to me, so similar to my cousins' house outside of London and the flats in which I had lived in Edinburgh that I felt immediate comfort the first time I walked in the house. His mother was delighted to have me there. The sofa in the living room was ten feet long and a dreadful gold. We spent a New Year's Eve on that sofa one year early on. We lay down after dinner, took a short nap, and about 9:30 p.m. woke up to decide we'd rather stay there than go to whatever party we'd been invited to. The Queen of Sheba painting hangs above the sofa and has been there for over sixty years. His sister hates it, and we love it. We have since replaced the furniture, even the carpet, with things I inherited from my parents, but the scantily clad Queen of Sheba remains in her place above the new sofa.

When Robbie graduated from high school, enlisted, left, mended soldiers, and came home, it was the English floral carpet, the gold sofa, and the Asian paintings above the twin beds in his room upstairs he left and came back to. I can't picture him as a little boy, but I can picture him leaving and coming home from Vietnam. His parents were told not to go to Oakland to meet him, something I hear all families were told. They, whoever "they" were, said that families shouldn't meet the troops. That's terrible. Robbie's parents had not seen their son for two years. He had just turned twenty and no one met him.

Robbie's father died three years after we met. We bought the house a few months later. I've never spent more than three months there at a time, but it is still home, a home with a history of mowing the lawn, barbequing steaks on the brick fireplace in the side yard, skinned knees, sister Mary's wedding gifts on display in the basement rumpus room, and of Kentucky in the horse pen by the garage on days their mother was going riding. It has a history of Seth spending every summer with his Granny Goose. It has a history of Robert and me going there for visits, family events, extended stays, and redecorating expeditions. Now that his mother is gone and it's just us there, I still find a sense of comfort knowing the dishes are still in the same cupboard, the silverware in the drawer, and the alcohol cabinet is below the silverware drawer. The workshop in the basement still has things of his father's—the tool chest, the fishing gear in the closet, and old paint cans probably quite dry inside.

In the upstairs hall closet, right where Robbie's father, George, left it so very many years ago, is the map of Vietnam. George marked it with the six different locations where his son served in those two years. It is one of the pieces of history I reverently touch, but never move, when I'm there.

In the basement is the closet of old clothes with the last of his uniforms remaining in the house. On our last trip, Robert decided it was time to get rid of his Class A uniform.

"Not before I take the ribbons and insignia off it," I said.

"Oh, don't put them in a frame and hang them somewhere in the house," he groaned.

"I won't. They just shouldn't be tossed away." *You earned them and paid dearly for them*, I thought. *They are a part of what has shaped the rest of your life.*

I took the service dress jacket upstairs to remove the ribbons and insignia. As I carefully unstitched the unit patch, I thought of the unit's motto, *vita ab morte* . . . life from death. The patch has five Greek crosses that refer to its five campaigns of World War II—Normandy, northern France, Rhineland, Ardennes-Alsace, and central Europe. It also represents a person's head, chest, viscera, and limbs, and the four elements of the universe—earth, air, fire, and water. Finally, it stands for substance, understanding, will, and wisdom. I always liked the motto and crosses on his shoulder patch.

I placed his patches, ribbons, and insignia in my top bureau drawer along with my hairbrush and scarves. This is the Alden bureau from one hundred years before this country was a country. It's the bureau I've had all my life. Everything has always been in the exact same spot. Now there is this addition of military insignia, newcomers to the bureau of a once-Quaker household. I'll find a good box to put them in the next time I go there.

Enlistment

We were young and naive.
He enlisted in the army
I enlisted in the marriage.

Welcome to the Army

I never wanted to be
the wife of
anyone.
I didn't mind marrying but
I wanted to be myself—
have a career, a child,
let my husband be the husband of. . . .

When I married a soldier, I didn't
know when I went somewhere
no one asked my name and SSN.
I, anonymous chattel owned
by the military, sat down and
without looking at me,
the clerk asked
What's your husband's SSN?

ii. Collateral Damage

Dying

When I was five, I had scarlet fever. In bed for three months, I ate oatmeal, toast with cinnamon sugar, and chicken soup, every day except for the week I lay unconscious with a 105.5-degree fever. Toward the end of my coma, I, in a prone position, lifted out of bed and floated past my mother and out the window. All the yellow spring flowers—daffodils, narcissus, jonquils, hyacinth, tulips, crocuses—bloomed on the snow-covered Massachusetts hillside. I went above the cirrus clouds between parallel columns of cumulonimbus clouds. I didn't want to go back, and when I did, I hovered at the window. Should I stay where I was? Should I go back, knowing how devastated my father's mother was at the loss of her three young daughters? My mother had told me those stories again and again. She always said she was so lucky to have her four children when my father had been the only survivor in his family. I went back.

My first words after a week-long silence were, "Mummie, what's heaven like?" After all, mothers know everything. My question threw her against the wall. She never answered me.

A month later, in April, I was well enough to have my tonsils out. I hemorrhaged. My sheets were damp and red. From my crib—there were no spare beds in the hospital—I watched the nurse look top to bottom and back again for sheets. The large cupboard was empty.

"Honey," she said, "Three boatloads of wounded just arrived in Boston and they requisitioned sheets from all area hospitals. We have no clean sheets. Either your parents can bring some or you can go home." I think it was a question, but I couldn't talk then or for the next three weeks. I didn't care what decision they made. I pictured those soldiers lying on boats. I already knew what pain and death felt and looked like. I was on their side.

You

You tell me you're OK because
You never saw combat but
You were blown out of bed and
You probably saw more dead in the OR
    than the fellow in combat
    unless he had a field of
    over five hundred to view.

Operating Room

Those in the operating room
Were too busy with incoming
Wounded and dying
to worry about incoming
mortars and missiles.
They cleaned
They cut
They sewed
Took out bullets and fragments
Scooped up innards or amputated legs
Put puzzle pieces back into faces.
Fell asleep twenty hours later
Too tired to weep.
So busy one day, some doctor assigned
a teenager to perform an appendectomy.

The Weight of

As he stands
in the OR
lifts the weight
of a dead body
off the table,
his hands,
gray,
detach from him.

I sit at my desk
reach my hands to its surface
stop above the life-
less body in the war zone's
surgery. I lift him
as my young pale hands
—immersed in aura—
shimmer,
detach from my arms.
He takes my hands with him
to float beyond today.

Collateral Damage

How many soldiers
did you see dying or dead
in frontline operating rooms
before you got laid for the first time
as a teenager on an R&R
in Bangkok?

Innocence Shattered

In memory of Jim Carlson

Out of uniform
he sat on the edge of his childhood.
Wept.
Shook
wept more.

Where is the boy who stood in the sand
in awe of the desert, ocean,
vastness of space?
He sits on the edge of his bed
mourning his friend.

Jim lay wounded—
he asked for Robbie.
The Army did what they could
to get his hometown buddy there, but
as Robbie walked to the helicopter word came

Jim had died.

Once home six months later,
he walked to visit the grieving mother.
Did he die for a reason, she asked.
He could not answer because there is
no reason in randomness.

He crept home, his soul too
weighted to walk, sat in the bathroom

three days sobbing.
What was its purpose? Why did he die?
Why do I live? His family,
not knowing what to do,
remained downstairs,
waited for him to get off the edge of his precipice,
waited for the boy they had sent to war to come home.
But the tears never dried. They just stopped
running down his cheeks.

Salt Licks

There has to be a better road
than to send young men—
flowers flourishing at the beginning of bloom—
to war
to return home to bawl like babies
or sob like a mother who has just lost her child.

I grow weary of tending my husband's tears
in buckets and jars around the house.

How Boys Become Men

When the soldier cries, he sheds no tears.

I.

Your mother thought you were a pyromaniac.
A friend assured her all boys are
until they turn into men
who build good fires.
Watch him stand before his primal flame.

Home on leave, you had your nineteenth birthday in Iraq.
You drive with an M-16 on the floor of the front seat
leaning up against the passenger door.
    Terrifying the town
    But no one asks you why

You stop your car to talk to me.
How good it is to see you,
How's your family? You ask.
How are you? I ask.
    I killed a twelve-year-old boy.
    It's good to be back.
    I killed a twelve-year-old boy.
    I'm home for two weeks.
    I killed a twelve-year-old boy.
    I'm going to the park.

Home on leave. A week ago you were in Baghdad streets
shooting at people, being shot at.

You did not leave those streets when you stepped off
the plane into the woods of Alaska.
What do you see behind the trees in the forests you played in as a boy?

You're nineteen. I weep for you
until you learn to weep for yourself.
Till then, World, hold him in the palm of your heart.

II.

Your mother tells me you guard a colonel.
That must be safe, I reassure her. No one's going to let anything
happen to a colonel.

Home on leave, you display six photos of buddies killed.
I sly a shot to your mother, mocking myself, as I slow my walk,
Seeing I was dead wrong.

Shot glass in front of each photo.
You place the seventh glass
—or is it the first—
in the middle before the unit emblem.

You fill each one.
Down a toast for your comrades from the shot glass in the middle.
Go to the first photo. Say something about him.
Offer a silent prayer. Pour his shot on the ground.
Down the row in one more farewell to each.
I wish their families could see you honor them.
I glance at my husband, a three-year two-war veteran—
your mentor you say, calling your mother from Iraq for his phone number.
Tears brim his eyes.

I went to Russia and Ukraine a month later.
Told several in both countries. Ah! The mothers nodded,
That is how our soldiers honor their dead in the field and once home:
Slavic tradition in a US Army platoon.

Mourn the dead
Bring the troops home.
I do not want to see mothers, sisters, wives, daughters,
brothers, fathers, and sons weep
Till they learn to nest their tears in the palms of their hearts.

Missing Faces

There are thistles
among
young daffodils.
Women
weep for faces
now gone.
History repeats
itself
when torn hearts ache.

Eight Months

with Elinor Veit

February 25, 1991

Monday

My dear cousin Abigail,

I was happy to get your letter about your different situation, so I waited to see what turn the war was taking. I am in sympathy with you having a husband in a war area but feel somewhat better that he is not in the front lines or any imminent danger. The news this morning tells us that things are going well for us and that the casualties are very light.

It is very possible that you saw my Robert in uniform. His ships would make port occasionally in Boston, and he would visit our Grandma Lichty in Jamaica Plain and take Aunt Blanche to dinner and a movie.

He was a lieutenant commander in the Navy and fought in the Korean War and World War II. Most of the time he commanded armed guard crews aboard oil tankers and made many trips to the Persian Gulf. In one convoy there was a ship sunk directly in front of his, and one directly behind. There was a period of over eight months when I did not have *any* idea of where he was, as the censorship was so heavy. I, too, know what it is like to be both mother and father to our children and having to make *all* the decisions.

Things went smoothly for many years after the end of the war and everything was peaceful, until Eric, our son, graduated from H.S. and joined the Navy. After Boot Camp at Great Lakes he was stationed aboard an aircraft carrier, the *USS Ticonderoga,* and spent three and one-half years off the coast of Vietnam.

Dear Abigail, hopefully this present conflict will be over soon, according to the signs, and your Robert will be home with you again.

In the meantime, keep the faith, and know that someone is thinking of you, and understands.

Your loving cousin,

Elinor

P.S. Keep in touch and let me know how things go. E.V.

Elinor was my rock. She is my cousin, and her children are my age. Yes, I remember seeing her Robert show up at the front door in his white uniform, a vision of loveliness and hope when he arrived and was shown so warmly into our home, the gathering place for any relative in need of companionship during the war or even a place to move into when a loved one was gone.

After her statement about not hearing from her Robert for eight months, everything suddenly seemed remarkably easier. *I can do this,* I thought, *however long it takes, whatever the outcome.*

31

In memory of the 31 lost in the helicopter crashes of August 2011

31 lost
31 doors
Receive that dreaded knock,
Unwanted visit
Leave families with shattered hearts
31 pairs of boots lined up with rifles and dog tags and helmets
Comrades grieved for and remembered
31 funerals
Names on newly made grave markers
31 empty places at the table
31 souls who gave all, whose deaths leave a void.
Take 31 days and months

                                    —Pause
                                    Reflect
                                    on—

Sacrifices of 31 lives gone forever.

Sleeping through the Night

A longtime family acquaintance and my mentor and friend for forty years, Ogden Lindsley was a B-24 flight engineer and top turret gunner during World War II. Shot down over the northern Albanian Alps in July 1944, he and the rest of the surviving crew arrived at Stalag Luft IV in Gross Tychow, Poland on his twenty-second birthday. On 6 February 1945, with the Russians advancing from the east, the Germans began to move their prisoners around the country in long columns. For sixty-seven days the men of Stalag IV walked three hundred miles to Stalag XI-B near Falling Bostel.

Lindsley was in a group of three POWs from his new camp sent under guard to gather wood. The Allies and Germans began to exchange gunfire. Seeing an opportunity to escape, he and the two Frenchmen ran toward the sound of the Allied guns while the German guards fired from behind them. Caught between the Allied and Axis shelling, the three men spent the night dug into the ground. Walking west the next morning, they froze as they heard a tank approach. When it rounded the bend, they saw, to their great relief, it was friendly. The hatch opened and a Brit stuck his head out to say, "Here, blokes. Have a smoke on me," and tossed them a tin of Gold Leaf cigarettes. Ogden kept the tin for the next fifty-nine years till he died. It is now in his archive. He told them to keep walking another mile to join the British Second Army RAF. Ogden, at six foot one, now weighed 115 pounds. The three men were sent to a food tent, then outfitted in British military gear. Soon after, they were transported to an RAF plane—with no chute, Ogden noted—and flown to GI Camp Lucky Strike near Brussels.

Much like the desire of other World War II veterans, Ogden's goal was to help improve how individuals learn, live, and interact. These men wanted to do what each could to avoid our world at war again. When Ogden returned home, he re-enrolled at Brown University to finish his undergraduate degree. He later became an experimental psychologist and leader in analyzing the behavior of people. He developed a unique measurement system, which he called precise behavior management, to help people monitor and change behavior. The system, now called precision teaching, embodies the broadest definition of teaching and learning.

Relaxing on the third floor of their home in the late 1990s, Ogden's wife, Nancy, found a magazine article about B-24 bombers. She went downstairs and gave it to him. He went on an Internet search for three days looking for his fellow crewmembers. Finally finding Richard Chancellor's number, Ogden called him. When the former pilot answered the phone, the former flight engineer said, "The last time I heard your voice, you said, 'Bail out.'" Chancellor told Ogden that that falling oil pressure crippled the plane and he, as flight engineer, had not erred in fuel transfer. Chance, the pilot flying the plane the day before, had redlined it. Short on planes, the Army Air Corps sent the unknowing next pilot on the alphabetical list, Chancellor, up with his crew for the final flight of the ill-fated plane. After hearing this news from his pilot, Ogden slept through the night for the first time in fifty-three years. Months later, Richard and Ogden saw one another for the second time in their lives.

No Win

Is it better to come home
to no thanks
Or to being thanked
for killing the enemy and losing friends?

Betrayal

A soldier's affair does more
than betray spouse
and family. He, or she, sends
all of us—active, retired,
reservists—and
spouses back to our bedrooms,
living rooms, on walks,
at dinner tables
to long conversations on
fidelity, marital health
and the status
of the relationship. One
more service to country
offered at the expense of
the trusting partner.

Dread

The hawser he drags
usually gags
voices of reality
until they begin timeless screams
circling
the clock face
as fast as a second
as slow as a week.

There is no respite from panic.

IEDs

I stopped by Mary Anne's house to pick up something. She is the mother of one of five from our town of 365 souls deployed to Iraq or Afghanistan. While there, I asked her how Chris was.

"Oh, fine."

"What's he doing now?" He had been part of a small group guarding a colonel, but I knew his military occupation specialty (MOS) had changed.

"He's still disarming IUDs."

"IED, Mary Anne! IED! Improvised explosive device. An IUD is an intrauterine device," I said, still laughing.

"Oh whatever," she replied.

It took her more than a year to tell Chris. I think she should have told him while he was still in Iraq; those fellows need all the humor they can get. When she finally told him, he looked at her, shook his head, and smiled slightly.

A few years have passed and Mary Anne and I still do not see one another without a chuckle. No hi, just a laugh or chuckle.

Someone's Brother

So you had an affair while
I was in the sand.
The least you could have done was

to meet my plane or
tell me yourself. No, I knocked
on the wooden door

now to surprise you
and our children, but some man
answered in his briefs, whiskey in hand.

Caution

I walked up behind a friend yesterday.
He did not jump, startle, or look astonished
but greeted me in a friendly manner.
I startled though.
Here was someone who was not alarmed
by my presence
behind him.

I take detours to approach
you from the front,
slow my walk or
cough from 20 feet away—
to give you time
to sense another's presence.
I never get a winsome smile
only a stare before we speak.
Then I see the cautions melt.

Returning

On return from Iraq
a captain camped on Kodiak
with fellow Marines,
kayaked Glacier Bay
a week alone,
came to my house to do
laundry and shower.

When my husband came home,
the captain asked "How long does it take?"
I stood in the kitchen and turned off
my ears.

This was a conversation between
two from combat
not one for eavesdropping.

Wall Drug

Deep in the desert, he stood by the sign
his face unshaved, weapon and mouth held slack,
stared into the lens of space. He would bless the absence
of emotion if he thought about feeling nothing.
His eyes pierce deep beyond pain and exhaustion,
Allow a film to sever him from the world's blindness.
I want to hold the five-year-old boy
you once were, soothe the open artery,
rock you and tell you it will all be all right,
watch you recover then leap from my lap
to run and play as if you never will
let any blood again.

A Parent's Pain

When he spoke of his son's return
home from his first tour, he teared, audibly choked,
turned his face sharply away from me.

The Stare

You stare at me
exhaustion—
the thousand-yard stare—
?
I don't know which
comes from your unshaven face
Are you home?
Do you remember who I am?

Will you ever return to the man I kissed goodbye?

Sleep

A small, orphaned Afghan girl
in an orange top and shorts
bears a half moon scar across her shaved scalp.
She sleeps against his shoulder and neck.
He sleeps, too, in a large blue soft plastic armchair
a bulk of an Air Force Master Sergeant who
comes every night to hold
the little girl who whimpers in anyone else's arms.
How do we understand love spoken only through touch
—across language and culture?
Does he have a daughter this age?
Will he dream about the little Afghan girl
as his child grows older?
How do we know whom to trust when we sleep?

Lullaby

This is a poem about a woman holding her infant,
clinging to a cliff.
Above her is a hungry, angry tiger,
below her the raging rapids of a deep river.

The mother has no choice but death for herself and her infant.
This is a song about her comforting her infant before they both die.
So too is this about the soldier who finds himself with no good choice.

Ee ya ee ya ee ya
Ee ya ee ya ee ya
Mmmm . . . mmmm . . . mmmm.
Ee ya ee ya ee ya

Uhhh!
Down.
Ahhh!
Floating

Kee-kaw. Kee-kaw.

Aye Yaaaaaaah!

The Deer Hunter

*A*s I lifted up the covers on my side of the bed, he said, "Don't touch me!"

I remember only one scene from the movie—a soldier sitting at a table in a bar in Vietnam. I need no sound to hear the background noise. I want to see the film again to understand its terror. I never want to see that film again.

I laid the covers down with extreme gentleness, but not until I'd said, "I'm going to lay the covers down now." The room was quiet. "Do you want me to sleep somewhere else?"

"I think that would be a good idea."

"I'm going downstairs."

I slept soundly for three hours, then woke with a start, sat straight up. Tentatively, I walked into the bedroom. I'm not sure what I said—Are you okay? How are you? Do you want me to sleep with you? Should I go downstairs again?—but I probably started off with the quiet announcement: It's Abigail, your wife. His response was clear. He lifted the covers, and I climbed in next to him. Still at the precipice, between the raging tiger and the deafening currents of some unknown river below, he grabbed me, bound his arms around me so he wouldn't fall again. I knew I shouldn't move, couldn't move, because I did not know what his response would be, and I did not want to put him back in Vietnam. I waited till I heard that calm breathing of sleep. Still he held me tightly and still I didn't move. Why disturb his escape. I fell asleep in his grip of desperation.

Touching Blood

for OJ, RG, BM, DF, JH, LD, and too many more

It is best to breathe
clean air
Run through fields
Ride your bike.
When you are six, you skin
your knee
Lick the blood clean

Taste it
Keep it from dripping.
When you go to the battlefield
at home or in country
You touch blood—

Your own
Your buddy's
Your best friend's—
You touch him
clamp a hole
hope he doesn't die.

When you work in a field hospital, you
touch, see, smell the blood
of hundreds of wounded. Taste
iron. Smell death in its steely
approach.

Watch a soldier
stop breathing
as you
try to save him.

You weep inside for
the rest of your life.

Comforting the Remnants of My Soldier

The rats of war
chewed pieces out of you.
I hold you at night
covering the holes with my skin.

iii. Robert and Abigail

The Man I Love

*H*e lies on his cot in a tent in Vietnam. He's eighteen, old enough to be in a war zone but not old enough to shave. He has not a hair on his chest. Incredibly youthful and handsome. A naive smile lights up his eyes, his mouth, his face, his life. I see a happy, young soul lying there, leaning on an elbow with his arms outstretched . . . waiting for me. Waiting for me to walk into his life. Waiting for me to hold him. He is waiting to close those arms around me. To love till death do us part. And beyond.

What he lost in Vietnam still makes me weep for the man I fell in love with when he came home.

The woman who framed the photograph for me looked at it and said, "He's a hottie."

"Yes," I smiled.

Part of a Soldier

I love the man you are,
was shocked to learn
I'll never know the one
Who lived inside your skin
before you went to war.

Does that mean I love only
part of you?

Never the Same

*F*orty years ago, I met a man home from two tours in Vietnam, resigned from the army. We had one of those experiences I don't believe in— love at first sight. Gratefully and miraculously, we're still married. I saw him re-up so he could afford to buy a Rototiller for the garden. He went from enlisted to officer and ten years later to Desert Storm. I now listen to the gratitude he gives for every retirement check. I see the "thanks for your service" he finally receives and feels. I see the healing of two men when soldiers or marines return, seek my husband out to spend time with him and perhaps ask, "How long does it take?"

Six months ago, his sister made a casual comment that he was never the same after he came home in 1969. I waited months till I saw her again to ask what she meant. Who was this man before Vietnam? Before I met him? Her husband blurted out, "About time we talk about this, fifty years later!" They said he was happy-go-lucky, gung ho, positive, and he offered a smile that would lighten a room or a soul.

In my twenties, I was too young to know the future I was marrying, the history of war I was about to live, but I know it wormed its way into our relationship long ago. I now know the healing is never complete, but life grows tolerable, pleasant, and fun again. I doubt there is a day I don't think about war and its soldiers, veterans, families on both sides, and, yes, my husband as a soldier.

Yesterday afternoon I asked, "Do you know tomorrow is Vietnam Veterans Day?"

"Yes. I heard that on the TV."

I could tell he felt thanked by the nation, and he seemed to have no regrets it didn't come sooner. He lives in the present. Even with the delay, I see the national attention make a miniscule dent in his dark side and am grateful.

I kissed him goodbye this morning with a, "Today is Vietnam Veterans Day," and another personal thank-you. As I sit on a plane flying over the town where we live and the Fairweather Mountain Range on my way to Fairbanks to receive an award for "Comforting the Remnants of My Soldier," I think of this. It is Vietnam Veterans Day. Why didn't we just welcome them home at the time? I'm glad they have designated a day, but it comes forty years after the fact.

Falling asleep as the plane taxied and took off, thoughts came to me. I miss the man I would have married. I am sad for the physically and emotionally disabled, grieve for those who died and left their families so permanently altered. I am sad that Robert saw so many people die. If his was the last face a person saw, the last caring eyes someone looked into, I am grateful for that, but he and his comrades paid a high price for those intimate moments of the departure of another's soul. I miss the calmness and peace, the simplicity that would have lived in my home or, more importantly, within him. I miss seeing the beam of his natural smile when it doesn't come for weeks.

I awake before I fall fully asleep because a rush of tears wells, and I don't want to cry in public. I absorb the moment and objectify the emotions.

He deserved more than my thanks. All those who've been to war deserve our deepest gratitude, the favors we can do for them, the care and consideration we can offer them.

I sometimes wonder who was the person I would have married if he'd never gone to war.

That day as I sat in the Anchorage airport waiting for the Fairbanks plane, I went to the web, then sent this email to him.

Sent: Friday, March 29, 2013 9:52 AM
Subject: Welcome Home!

Hi Sweetie,

http://www.alaskapublic.org/2013/03/28/

vietnam-veterans-day-signed-into-law/

This is what I found at the website when I Googled Vietnam

Veterans Day. Evidently tomorrow is the fourth annual one in the

country, but today is the day the last troops left and Alaska's first

Vietnam Veterans Day.

Welcome home, Sweetie. I'm glad you're here and glad we met.

I love you.

Love,

Abigail

Although we had talked on the phone, this morning I received his reply.

Sent: 4/2/13 24:15 AM

Subject: Re: Welcome Home!

Thanks for your support. See ya at 5:30 tomorrow. Love, Rob

Once again, I had tears in my eyes. I know he's said thank you to me many times before about many things, but he's never written it or said it in that way. That's the sentence I sometimes hear from a soldier when I talk to him or pay for his coffee in person. Yet from my husband it seemed so terribly personal. He wasn't just thanking me for my comment about the day. I felt in that one simple sentence he was thanking me for forty-three years of being together and loving one another no matter what.

Army Wife

I am an Army wife
Felt it when
he was about to deploy.
I headed the Family Support Group.
Forgot who I was when he came home.

I am an Army wife.
Realized it again when I began to write this.
Tucked the reality and thought inside.

You are an Army wife, a friend said.
—What a lovely compliment—

You're right, I am.
He may hide his dark side, but
I can no longer pretend its absence.

He does all the daily practical things.
In exchange
I cover his invisible wounds at night
as we cuddle
because I am his Army wife.

Husband

Husband:

Last week, my husband said, "I was enlisted to kill in Vietnam and Iraq."

Some parts of his service he tells with pride:

"I never killed anyone. I never fired my weapon at anyone."

"I'm a Major."

"I retired with 28 years."

"I did three tours."

"One time I worked 37 hours straight in surgery in Vietnam."

Four years ago he said, "I'll never know all the issues Vietnam brought up for me. I'll live with them unresolved."

Other people:

He is a gentle soul, a compassionate person.

Wife:

He is gentle, shy, and terribly funny much of the time.

He's practical while I live in my head or on another planet.

Differences

*F*riends sometimes ask what brought Robert and me together. Robert Strasser, a German exchange student who lived with us for a year when he was seventeen and Seth was fifteen, recently put it this way: "I never came to ask what brought these two utterly different people together and made them stick." He wondered then how different my husband and I were and what were the attractions and glue that kept us moving forward.

The initial attraction on both our parts was appearance that spoke beyond the physical. I saw he was athletic and tied to the earth even before he stood in front of me. My first glimpse of him was a man comfortable with his run. Nor was he out of breath when he arrived to stand before me. He was driving a truckload of cattle. Not too many intellectuals or businessmen do that, not that I have any objection to either of those, but for a long-term relationship, they had not passed muster. His attraction to me was that I, like most pregnant women, glowed. He also glimpsed a level of responsibility and independence, a pregnant woman whose husband wasn't hovering over her.

When he came in my house to use the phone, he expressed amazement at the Persian carpet, baby grand piano, books on the shelves on either side of the fireplace, paintings on the walls, without commenting on any one item. This was a world foreign to him, but he described it as a beautiful home.

Before the evening ended, we saw and heard more about each other. We each liked and felt more comfortable in nature than in town. I lived thirty miles out of town in a cabin in the woods next to the river. He lived even farther upriver and had grown up in ranch country. We liked solitude and didn't mind spending time alone. He saw my house was neat and clean.

He saw I was seven months pregnant. I told him I had grown up back east in a large house in a suburb of Boston and in New York's Greenwich Village. I had a master's degree, and he'd been to war not college.

We heard and saw one another's work ethic. He worked at McKenzie-Willamette Hospital in surgery and was driving cattle for his version of fun. He spoke of his desire to always be money ahead. I told him I was taking a month off after my baby was born, then going back to work full-time at the university in Eugene. There was no mention of my husband, but it was apparent he was nowhere around.

There were incomprehensible aspects of a possible relationship, one being his military duty and my being a Quaker, although less a believing one then than I am now. He came from an Irish Catholic family. I came from a Boston suburb where you either were Irish and Catholic or you were not. We were not. I grew up in big cities, he in ranch country. I saw he was practical and knew I was not. I think he told me he'd never read a book outside of school nor listened to classical music, both passions of mine. He was excruciatingly and wonderfully practical; I walked around with thoughts and feelings that ranged to outer space.

Just yesterday, I received a message from our German exchange student responding to some of my writing from this book that is at Scroll in Space, an online literary journal. After I read his message, I burst into sobs that would not stop. I sat at my desk sobbing and sobbing about . . . I had no idea what other than . . . I don't know. I couldn't put it into words. I remember trying to figure out . . . there were no thoughts, and I accepted that there would be none. I have a note posted above my desk that a friend sent me a week ago. "Methinks you try to analyze everything too much. Just get up and say good morning, not that the Earth made another revolution while screaming through space." At that moment of continuous sobbing, I knew my friend's words were there and had a glimpse of possible practicality for the first moment in my life. When I stopped sobbing, I said "good morning" to his words and the spruce forest outside my window. Maybe I can be more practical just not very often.

Robbie and I would learn later that he was very punctual, and I was as tardy as they come. Arguments came that still exist to this day, although I try to be better for him, and he tries not to worry about time or yell about it so much. We had yet to learn that there were two people with tempers in this relationship. In kindergarten our son wrote a story about me for Mother's Day. He wrote, among other usual things, "My mommy takes long showers," and, "My mommy yells at my daddy a lot." Golly, I thought Robert yelled at me a lot.

I remember Robert saying that he wanted a woman who was comfortable enough with herself that the two of them would have cabins on opposite sides of the hill. She would live in one and he in the other. *Naive and odd*, I thought, *but he will learn otherwise.*

To others, we seem to have no common interests. He's a nurse, and I can barely figure out when to take a pill for pain. When Seth and my niece, Abi, still lived at home, they'd come to me when they'd really hurt themselves or were in pain. Me? I'm the one who says to go get a Band-Aid or wait awhile and you'll feel better. Children usually go to their mother for help with accident or illness but not in this family. If they wanted a discussion, they came to me. Robert gave black and white answers for illness, car keys, and everything else. I analyze everything, plan, then do. He analyzes nothing and acts immediately. I am proper and follow the rules. He was wild then, less so now. But he still doesn't always follow the rules. Nor do I any longer. Does that make him a practical person, someone in the medical field, or someone who's been at war? All of the above.

There were, of course, elements in common that underlay the relationship. We both had PTSD but didn't know it. Indeed, its definition and clinical diagnosis wouldn't appear for another ten years. We each knew there were elements of discomfort within our own skin, but neither of us yet knew how to put those weird and angular pieces into words. Somehow, though, we sensed that amorphous sphere that floated within and between us, or the relationship never would have lasted. We both have a strong sense of loyalty, which would be necessary as the years passed.

Most of our differences still exist, but we have learned not to criticize the other for those habits. I've learned to keep my mouth shut . . . most of the time. He has learned to say, "Yes, dear."

Opposites

He, *Penthouse* subscriber—I, poet
Coming from work at 2:00 a.m.—getting up at 4:00 a.m.
Diving into the inner tube in the Kansas River—
swimming daily 6:00 a.m. in the pool
Beer anytime—five o'clock tea
He, much more withdrawn, I open and talkative to everyone
He the more observant individual

Tries not to touch his boundaries,
holds himself carefully,
afraid someone might see his dark side.
I am the opposite, still a little girl who hasn't
Learned to leave some risks alone.

Together

Mutual love of nature
Still attracted to one another
The bedroom is time for us where
we allow no talk of issues
Honor one another
Laugh—
All and more pulls us through
my intensity and his dark moments.

The Husband of...

*W*hat does he say of me? In years gone by I remember that he thought I was always late, panicked without cause, and didn't do the dishes often enough. I didn't always want to make love when he wanted to and didn't initiate family activities but waited till he did. When we met, he liked me because I was intelligent, independent, could take care of myself, and had a good income. He tells me that about once every five years. I knew he wanted someone sane and reliable and that he didn't want to marry someone like his mother.

Today he says I snore some nights and leave the compost in the kitchen drain. I guess if those are my only two faults, we're okay. I still have a punctuality problem, but I'm better, and he doesn't yell at me for being late anymore. I have another problem, though. Last summer, I thought I'd do my son a favor and fuel up his truck that was very close to empty before I drove his children, Norah and Reid, home. I wasn't sure I'd make it out to his place and he'd be able to make it back to town. *I'll fill it up . . . No, I'll just put a gallon in it. It's his work truck, and that's a business expense.*

Having put a gallon in and feeling self-righteous, I drove seven-eighths of a mile to the post office before the five-mile trek to his place. I pulled into the parking lot and realized I'd just put gasoline in a diesel truck. I asked someone there what I should do. Don't start it. It needs to be towed and the tank drained. Norah and Reid sat very silently in the back with no laughter, tickling, or talking. I called Seth, but he did not answer. I left a message and burst into tears. I called the fellow who would tow it, drain it, and make sure all was good. Of course, that would be on my dollar.

Norah spoke, "It's okay, Granny. Daddy won't be mad. It was just a mistake. He'll understand." While I liked her five-year-old reasoning, I wasn't sure it was accurate. Seth was not happy when he called me back as I still sat in the truck in the post office parking lot. My daughter-in-law, Kezia, then called me to tell me how she and I would resolve the current transportation crisis. I misunderstood her and thought I'd have to walk the children the mile and a half to Seth and Kezia's office. Right, a five-year-old and a three-year-old really want to go for a mile-and-a-half walk with their crying granny. "No, you stay there," she said, "I'm coming to get you."

Officially, I had panicked. I couldn't come up with a solution. I didn't understand the solutions others offered. Robert must have been in Juneau at work and on med rounds. He's my go-to person when I panic. In the twenty years from the late '70s to the '90s, when I was a public school principal of a preschool through high school for disturbed children or of a regular elementary inner city school, and there was a bad situation—a student hitting a teacher or trying to throw me onto the ground or armed and threatening to come kill some of my students—I always remained calm and levelheaded. I was in charge, knew what to do, and had no choice but to remain the leader and clear thinker. On my own, though, Robert is my go-to guy. When I panic and think incoherently, he tells me what to do. He never behaves like Major Giese then. He's calm and quietly takes charge. But here I was, on my own and taking care of my grandchildren. That seems simple enough, right?

When he came home several days later, he cocked his head, smiled, and said, "There's no Navy Seal in you."

Getting Along

A sat at the mahogany table where I had eaten breakfast, lunch, and dinner, Thanksgiving, Christmas, and all birthday dinners as a child. My mother gave the table to me, and it is in my dining room now. I was reading the paper or paying the bills when Robert walked up, paused long enough to put something on the table, and said, "I don't know how two people get along in a relationship when I have so much difficulty getting along with myself." I looked up, but he was not looking at me. He continued on into the living room or upstairs.

Years later I asked him a question as he walked downstairs while buttoning his shirt.

"Can't you see I'm busy?" he replied.

I didn't laugh, but remembered when we were at the landfill one time. We asked the dump master a question. He said, "I'm sorry. I can't sort these cans, listen to your question, and see who's driving by." Turning to me, he continued, "You women can multitask, however."

"Of course we can," I said. "The baby would die if we couldn't take care of him and stir the soup pot at the same time."

Multitasking: the ability to do more than one behavior at a time because both, or all, are so fluent, none requires thought. I would think walking, talking, and buttoning are all fluent behaviors in an adult. What if he was thinking something else, though?

Flowers

*R*obert has worked as a nurse in the prison in Juneau for sixteen years. One evening while at work, Robert was sitting in the cafeteria with Jeannie, a probation officer, and one of the correction officers at the prison. Jeannie was unusually cheerful as they ate. When she got up to put her tray where the finished ones go, Robert, who had never seen her smile before, asked the other fellow at the table why she was so happy. "I don't know, ask her," he said. Robert did.

"I'm getting a divorce," she replied gleefully.

A few days later, when I stepped off the jet from a consulting trip, Robert met me at the airport with flowers. He came home the next day . . . with more flowers.

I had received flowers when Seth was born. Other than that, he bought me rose bushes when we lived in Kansas, which I usually planted.

After his new behavior, I asked him why the sudden change. "I don't want you getting a divorce from me, and worse, being happy about it."

Since Jeannie's divorce ten or twelve years ago, he continues to bring home flowers every other week when he returns from Juneau. Lilies, irises, carnations, roses, alstroemeria, tulips, or whatever else is available at the grocery store. It's always a surprise, because I never know what he'll bring. Alstroemeria is a Peruvian lily, which lasts forever, often beyond his next arrival with more flowers. In the long dark winters of Alaska, flowers brighten the house. On rainy fall days that seem to stay gray forever, I appreciate them. On sunny days I like them, too. They last longer than wildflowers, and I can leave those outside to look at on walks around our place or in the woods.

Which are my favorites? The ones that come every other week. Not long ago, he brought home some floribunda roses, the kind that has many flowers on one stem. These were orange rimmed in pink and there were fifty-four little roses on seven stems. The ones in my study are drying beautifully. I'll save them because I'm a sentimental person.

Sometimes he says he can drink when he wants because he brings me flowers each time, but he knows that's not true. At least I hope he does. Other times he says that we always get along for the first half of the week that he's home, but by the time he has to go back, we're both ready for a week off from one another. Maybe, but that's not really true either. It's certain, though, that when he arrives home, we're really glad to see one another, and I appreciate his gift of flowers.

Intimacy

*R*aised a Catholic, Robbie lost his desire to go to church and confession sometime in Vietnam. It was the first time he saw a different religion: Buddhism with its tranquility and peace. He went to talk to the Catholic priest about questions of war, its morality, and what was he doing there. The priest was an army chaplain and gave him what I call "the party line"—we are here to serve our country, fight Communism, protect the people of South Vietnam, and other noble causes. The priest he was used to, though, was from Ireland and tied to the community of Robbie's predominantly Irish hometown in eastern Oregon. He seemed a local and was the person you could talk to about anything. My husband has not gone to confession or communion since he returned from Vietnam. He still crosses himself when in church for a family event and after the blessing at mealtime.

His confessions now are to me. I know much, perhaps too much, about his missteps in life. We stood in the living room one day talking. Along came some tale of something he'd done. Whatever it was, this one seemed a simple issue to me, but, suddenly, it felt like the priest would have been the better person to tell.

"Say five Our Fathers and ten Hail Marys," I said. He immediately had the loveliest smile of surprise. I still get the confessions. We share our joys and accomplishments of each day, too. I guess that's what best friends are.

One year he offered something precious to us as a family. When our son and niece were teenagers, he had three jobs—surgery nurse, psychiatric nurse, and nurse in the Army Reserves. I was a principal. He saved us from being a family of ships passing in the night. He insisted we set aside an hour a week for an activity together. It couldn't be a meal, watching TV, or going to a movie. We already did all those things. This activity had to be interactive. We played board or card games on the living room floor, went for walks, sat and talked in front of the fire, and whatever we did in those three years almost always lasted all afternoon or evening.

Intimacy comes in many forms. It has been in the relationship since we met. In the six months before we invaded Iraq in 2003, however, it began to deepen to a level without words. Any behavior has thirty to forty reasons for its occurrence. I can think of only some reasons why our relationship changed. If he weren't retired from the military, he could be one of the ones going. We knew about families that are separated. We felt concern for our country and theirs. He said it would turn out to be another Vietnam with little justification for our presence. We believed the inspector who accurately reported there were no WMDs or plants to build them left in Iraq. Perhaps he felt the fear and excitement that any soldier feels as he leaves for a battleground. Certainly I felt the fear of the wife, mother, and family left behind.

Intimacy. We have ties that bind us to one another, lines as secure as ones that fasten a boat to dock or a ship at anchor. Perhaps that line is a ribbon or even the flag. Perhaps it was the knowledge that after thirty-three years in this relationship by 2003, we did not want to lose so much as one more day of it. Was it the fear of what war would do to him again? To us? Maybe it was just too much emotion to bear. Maybe it's that we felt the thousands of families going through this separation, thousands of men and women gone from their families and countries. Perhaps for him it was all the military and civilian casualties and damage that would occur, including the war surgeries he had seen far too many of.

Whatever the reasons, ever since the invasion of Iraq, we hug more often. We cling to one another at night. When I put my arms around him, I cover the physical wounds he never got. I cover the wounds of those he mended in surgery or those who fought in more recent wars. I cover the wounds that make his heart ache or startle him in the day.

Our lovemaking returned to the level of our twenties and the newness of the relationship. How else do a man and a woman become close without words? I get up between 4:00 and 5:00 a.m., except on the weeks when he's home. Then I stay in bed and we hold one another as we sleep or talk. One day after lunch, I suggested a third hop in bed. His response, as he was about to go downstairs and outside, was, "Oh go call someone else. I want to go outside."

News events we hear on the radio make us both stop to listen. We talk a lot more about his experiences, and I feel free to ask some questions in response or out of the blue. We move from the topic of war to what's for supper. We now make passing comments without kerfuffle about Vietnam, news events, or soldiers. We stopped socializing so much, wanting just one another's presence.

I want to take the eighteen-year-old I never knew into my arms, the nineteen-year-old, the twenty-year-old, the eighteen-year-old boy who left for Vietnam, the twenty-year-old man who returned, the twenty-one-year-old man I met, the twenty-one-year-old I loved. I want to take every historical moment of you into me and hold you there in that moment—forever in those moments, all moments at one time. I want to hold you in the palm of my heart, clutch you within me.

I want us to cling together as if we might lose one another. I want to give as much of me as possible, I want to get as much of you as possible. I want the intimacy of oneness stored up before we are separated by death.

I picture the intimacy of being with him at the Vietnam Wall. I've gone three times, but alone. I could control myself, barely the last time. He has not gone. When we were in DC, we went to my niece's father's and uncle's graves. We were on our way as a large family to my mother's funeral. One of us asked Robert if he wanted to go to the Wall while we were in DC. He said this trip had enough death without going there.

I can picture being there with him. I blink, glance to the side, then raise my eyes to the sky, anything to keep tears from flowing when standing there with him. It doesn't work for me, and he makes no effort to avoid his tears. I watch him stand alone, even turn away for moments to offer him his privacy until we wrap ourselves in one another's arms and weep. He will weep for the many souls he saw leave. We will weep for his innocence lost so brutally. We will weep for the changes to our life together that we still do not comprehend. Oblivious to others milling about, no one is there but us; we are surrounded by The Wall.

iv. Deployment

410th to Deploy

*R*obert may have been in the US Army Reserves, but *reserves* can be a relative term. We both knew the army could call him back to active duty any time they wished. We were apprehensive when Saddam Hussein invaded Kuwait and became more so when we learned that his unit was one of twelve medical units on the list for call to active duty with 72-hour deployment notice. Still, we waited from early August till late November.

The call came at Thanksgiving time. The 410th Evacuation Hospital with its four hundred personnel was to leave the following week for Fort Riley. I don't remember what day it was, but I clearly remember when I answered the phone and it was Top, the top sergeant in the unit. I recognized his voice immediately and knew why he was calling. This was the 72-hour notice.

The Saturday after Thanksgiving, a reporter from the *Topeka Capital-Journal* showed up at drill to interview some of the troops. Robert, in a move very unlike him, went up to the reporter and said, "I'm the guy you want to talk to."

He was one of the unit's few who had served in Vietnam. He also had a unique reason for enlisting in the army a second time: he wanted a Rototiller that we couldn't afford. Such patriotism.

I'm not sure which amazed me more—that he had re-upped or that he had volunteered to share his story with the reporter. The *Topeka Capital-Journal* published the article on the front page on 22 November 1990. The paper included the Rototiller story along with the other details of the unit's call to deploy:

The 410th also needs people like Capt. Robert Giese, who normally works as a rehabilitation nurse at St. Francis Hospital. He also works part time at Topeka State Hospital.

Giese got his first combat medical experience as an operating room technician with a MASH unit in Vietnam. When he left the Army in 1969, he expected that to be his last time in Army greens.

But he joined the Army Reserve in 1974 for an unusual reason.

"I wanted a Rototiller. I couldn't afford it. So I joined the reserve for the money," he said.

Giese decided he liked the reserve, even after he bought his garden tool. He joined the 410th in 1977 when he moved to Topeka.

We still have the Rototiller. It's on the north side of one of the barns at his sister and brother-in-law's ranch. Grass grows up around it as it sits like a piece of old farm equipment, a once-functional item and now a relic. I think we should put it in the side yard at 708, a rusting talisman decorating the lawn at the house where he grew up, left for war, and returned.

He said he joined the Reserves for the Rototiller money, but he stayed for another twenty-six years. It was more than just the money, but he'll never say so.

A Sliver in Protocol

I interviewed some Coast Guardsmen for a book I wrote about a commercial fishing accident and rescue. One of them was surprisingly formal, addressing me as Ms. Calkin for four years. His fellow officers and enlisted men called him "by-the-book" or "1A and squared away." Occasionally, his formality fractured, such as when he described the skipper tangled in the lines, his feet barely reaching the deck as he stood on "his tippy toes."

I know these tough men and the momentary crack in the surface. With my husband's 72-hour notice to deploy to Desert Storm, he flew into a flurry of activity. I stayed out of his way until he hollered, "A watch! A watch! I need a watch!" I went to my jewelry box and handed him the one he'd given me twenty years earlier after his father's funeral. He looked at it resting on my palm. "Something might . . . I might lose it," he whispered. He stiffened as if he were wearing his Class A uniform, not his civvies.

"I do not want to take my father's watch to war," he said, as he turned a 180 and left the room. His language so precise, his manner so formal, so unlike him, he left me staring at the watch as his words and behavior reverberated against our bedroom walls.

As tough as they seem, I feel honored that they're not afraid to let me see beneath the crust.

I Do Not Want to Take My Father's Watch to War

Here is a watch, I said helpfully. No,
something might . . . I might lose it, you whispered,
then announced
I do not want to take my father's watch to war.

You were 17 when you volunteered
for Vietnam, one day out of high school,
20 and trembling when you came home.
We drove through clear-cut mountains
with the baby asleep in the car. I asked
What was it like?
You spoke a sentence or four quietly but clearly,
till your voice cracked, your hands shook.
Tears came as you flailed away
images unknown to me:
I do not want to talk about it anymore!

When our son was 17, we sat at the table
listening for three hours as you told us
your life in the Montagnard hills . . .
names, whelming surgical details, friends.
In the Delta you played volleyball
between surgeries.

I took the list Suggested Items for the Desert

to feel some part of your life
unknown to a Quaker.
Don't forget the volleyball, you said
You found it, pumped it, flattened it,
stuffed it in the duffel bag.

Will I see you before you go to the desert?
Will you come back alive, please?
Do I give your father's watch to our son
at a flag-draped funeral and say
This belonged to your Grandfather Giese?

Meeting Theresa

A notice in the school district announcements caught my eye. It asked for writings regarding Operation Desert Shield. I called the person who made the request: Theresa Hammett Steinlage. Yes, she was interested in anything I wrote, she said, as we struck up a friendship. Deciding a phone call was not enough, we agreed to meet after work at the Steak & Ale for something to eat. She got there first, not unusual since I'm late for almost everything. By this time, Robert was already stationed at Fort Riley.

Theresa and I sat at the bar drinking tea and snacking on a light supper. I told her how Robert ended up finding himself deployed to Desert Storm. She laughed. Her husband was in nursing school at the time and read the front-page article to her about this crazy situation of a guy who had enlisted fifteen years ago for a second time to buy a Rototiller and was now off to war for a second time. She told me about her father being in World War II and one of her brothers in Vietnam.

Like my friends, Ed and Onecia, and my cousin Elinor, Theresa immediately became another strong support for me. I was in new territory and needed people who had some familiarity with the emotional aspects of being the relative of a deployed military person. I met Ed and Onecia two years before I met Theresa. Ed, Onecia, and I were among the original members in the Topeka writer's group, Table for Eight. Theresa joined the group later. Onecia was also a teacher and Ed a Vietnam veteran. All four of these friends knew when to call or show up without being asked. That evening, I added Theresa to my list of supporters.

Christmas Day

He was at Fort Riley, due to leave any time for Desert Storm. At the last minute, the troops were told they could have a twenty-four-hour leave. He was one of the lucky ones who lived close enough to come home. He requested a tree. Robert never wants a Christmas tree. I remember sitting at the table for dinner, but I don't remember what we had—maybe homemade soup and sandwiches.

All I remember of that day is a tree in the living room with no decorations, or maybe we hung the lights and a few bulbs early in the evening at his request. I sat on the davenport and he next to the tree opposite me, each of us holding cups of homemade hot chocolate. We looked at one another in the light of many candles.

I don't remember sleeping with him Christmas Eve or night, but to have him home that day made it the finest Christmas I ever had.

Homefront

Ed Mercer

I saw a friend to war today
Then left him mending men
Half-stepping home
Feet as heavy as my head
I wish I had told him . . .
Wish I had said . . .
I hope he knows my heart.

Because
I've never waited for a soldier
To win a war or die
Like some of those who've clasped their hands
And bowed their heads to cry.

What else does one do?
Burn a candle? Tie a ribbon?
My stars already fly
But my stripes should do more
    Maybe I will shine my boots
    And clean a weapon
    The way I did before
In those simple days
When others waited.

Blinders

Brown leather blinders—
Drive the block ahead.

Thank God the road hasn't changed.
Red light—
Turn left when green. Turn left when green . . .
A horn blasted.

Oh.
I'm still here
He is gone.

Let me cry against your pillow when
I get home from work.

I haven't changed the pillowcase:
It still smells of you.

Notes from My Journal, August 1990–May 1991

Robert is a captain in Army Reserves, in a medical unit that is one of twelve in the country on 72-hour call. He told me yesterday that there are four times as many medical reservists as active duty. I told him I'd send letters telling him how the back yard was, the house, the animals, and Seth, that I wanted letters of the desert, the terrain, the people . . . descriptions of the Middle East. I can accept that Robert is going but don't like it one bit.

I feel anxious and depressed. He does not want to go: his income would be cut in half, he just had an irregular EKG, and he fears the disruption to home life. I do not want to be here alone, responsible for everything. If he goes, I need to make some changes—simplify, cut back on spending, add a half dozen duties he does and take away some of the things I enjoy.

Robert, Seth, and I had a terrible row Sunday night. I started it, and Seth got the brunt of it. The anxiety is awful, at least for me. I am depressed, upset, and distraught.

The Capital Journal had an article that the 410th (and eight other units) may be called. It doesn't help that Seth leaves this weekend for college two thousand miles away.

Seth left yesterday and for the first time it was difficult, for I realized that he will never again be home for longer than two to three weeks.

Ed Mercer, a soldier friend who was in Vietnam, and I went to Tanglewood yesterday. We took our dog, Willoughby, and walked around the lake.

I am having a very hard time going to Boston. In forty-nine years, this will be my first trip there alone and to visit no one. I miss my mother terribly and cry very easily. Old aches, like the pain in the back of my head and neck that used to make me black out, have returned.

Robert's unit has been placed on alert status. I am numb and exhausted. I never thought of myself as a military wife. I am, though. Very much so. I am the wife of a captain.

I feel as unmotivated as a tree.

The newspaper says, "The 410th provides hospitalization within combat zones," and that several members will report to the unit to prepare for activation. Hopefully, they won't leave prior to Thanksgiving.

Robert's unit is being activated 21 November, Wednesday. They go to Fort Riley 27 November, Tuesday and then to the Gulf three weeks later. I think he was not supposed to tell me all that.

We called Seth, Mary (Robert's sister), and Eleanor (his mother) Saturday and Sunday. I called Abi who called Hannah who called Mary and Bill. My siblings all called yesterday.

Onecia was coming over because I had called to ask her to. Ed told her to wait and he fixed three plates of food. His comment: Abigail hasn't eaten today. Oh, how right he was.

My sister, Mary, continues to send cards often. It feels so supportive. Hannah said she lives alone and does all those tasks by herself all the time. What was I upset about? My brother was concerned about his Volvo. What planet are those two on? Not mine or Robert's. I can rely on my in-laws, my son, sister Mary, a cousin, Ed and Onecia, and a few of the other wives. That seems like a lot, but there's a hole there named Robert.

December 25th

Robert is home for Christmas and how wonderful that is. I could not ask for a better present. We each gave one another nothing but care and affection this year. That is more than sufficient.

When he comes home, I will devote my life to him, for time is so precious. All this has renewed our relationship in a most pleasant and loving way.

I can last for about three days, no, two without hearing from Robert. On the third day of not hearing from him, I go crazy. I worry, become depressed and tearful, panic, even think I'll never see him again. My emotions are like the stock market and the price of crude oil—up and down, up higher and down lower, up and down.

Robert is fully aware that he joined the army and has a duty to do. I do not respect the men and women who have suddenly decided they are conscientious objectors. One doctor re-upped five days before Iraq invaded Kuwait, and within the week she became a conscientious objector. They joined the military whose function and purpose is war, be it defensive or offensive. Now that the potential is present, sergeants and doctors who have been in for a while suddenly are conscientious objectors. It doesn't work that way. Being a conscientious objector is a lifetime, moral commitment. Seth is one whether he realizes it or not. He refused to fight in the sixth grade when one of his best friends threatened him. In college, he refused to hit another friend when his friend beat him up so badly he was in bed for two days. Even I, his mother, would not have recognized him on the street. *That* is the position of a conscientious objector.

Uncle Bud died recently, and Seth learned he had been a lieutenant colonel in World War II. I don't think that will make him change his mind, though. He's coming home for a few days to see Robert before he leaves, so necessary for both of them . . . just in case. It's a positive, healthy statement about how much Seth cares for and respects him, and his presence here under these circumstances will mean a lot to both of them. Seth is still recovering from his almost fatal bicycle accident. His helmet saved his life. It is wonderful to have him here, to watch them interact. He has chosen to take the bus back in order to have more time here with his father.

Robert arrived home this afternoon with food poisoning. It was as if I finally had an explanation for why I felt so depressed all morning. I never showered or dressed till afternoon and have been close to tears several times since.

I seem to be getting used to this chaotic life, but I wish I knew where I put my military ID. I lost one of the dining room knives, too. And a fork.

Before Robert left for Fort Riley, he said that if he dies he feels it will be for a cause. He's going over there to help others; he is serving his country. It will not be for naught. He's appreciative to me for getting him through nursing school—for the life we live and have lived. He and we have done well and if he dies, his life is in a good place and his death is justified. It was hard to say goodbye today for I shan't see him again before he leaves.

I don't want to be a forty-nine-year-old widow. My years with him have been the twenty best of my life.

My nerves are raw, my stomach upset. My actions are slowed. I sit staring. I am simultaneously anxious and depressed. I wish he would call, for I want to hear his voice; I don't want him to call for the news will be bad.

War started yesterday evening. I was at a Japanese restaurant with Lynne and Terri (two of the 410th wives who talked me into being chair of the 410th Evacuation Hospital's family support group) and their children when we heard the news.

Now it's over, and I'm ready for Robert to come home today.
My mind is dulled. Hit by a rocket, it fizzles constantly with a background of nagging and poking anxiety. I wish to return to normal immediately, but realize that is impossible till Robert returns home safely. It's like having cramps every day, all day and night, and not being able to take anything.

The pain is sharp or dull but always present. It has taken over. The personal anguish is so great it blocks any creativity.

Depression: the slowing of activity.

I feel in danger for I cannot even escape into writing, my one sanctuary. I am frustrated and depressed trying to edit the manuscript of *Nikolin* and sink more into the quagmire rather than coming out of it.

Once again I felt Robert in bed with me and was surprised on waking how far away he is. Just now I was trying to think, *I don't want to go to work,* but instead twice I said, "I don't want to go to war."

I am exhausted and work is too long each day, too many hours, too tiring.

I went out to get the paper this morning. Moisture hangs in the air. Every now and then I heard a drop fall, probably water from a leaf that held all it could before brimming over. I heard no traffic. The world sleeps.

Robert called this morning shortly before, or after, 6:00 a.m. It was wonderful to hear his voice. He sounded so close that I thought he was lying next to me in bed. He said when he heard mine, he started crying and had difficulty talking. He said the fellows had given him a bad time about not calling home.

Deployed

Because I am not with you
I am sucked into the foggy
maelstrom.

Because I am with you
I ask you to pass the salt.
You hand it to me.

The magenta,
white and purple flowers you sent
cast shadows
strong as tree limbs against
the wall of our home

You put gas in my car, tell me to come in
out of the snow, remind me why
I walked into this room.

I think of you and hear the Chieftains
. . . or is it that I hear the Chieftains, and
think of you . . .

Because I am with you
we talk about the trees of the forest
as the back of my hand
curls into the palm of yours.

Because I am not with you . . .
you send me
whispers of your love
against my shoulders,
the touch of your words
on my fingertips.

Phone Calls

The phone rang as I unlocked the door.
Hello. It could have been the Wichita general
or a family member from
my husband's unit. It was. My mother-in-law wanted
to know if I was home. We laughed. I looked—
eleven messages waiting.
How was your day? How was yours?
Neither of us had heard from Robert.

Listened to the messages. Mostly questions about the jeep
that crashed in the desert.
Called the general for a fact check.
Was it our jeep? He hadn't heard;
he'd let me know. I called the wives and
mothers back. The general is checking.
I'll let you know. I could have waited but they
would only grow increasingly nervous with silence.

Fixed supper. Sour cream, salsa, and chips,
a carrot too. I went to the basement
turned on the TV.
The phone rang as
I watched the news from Iraq.
My mother-in-law calling again.
We watched part of the news together,
talking during muted commercials.

Lynne called. What about the jeep? Don't know yet.
Waiting to hear from the general. I'll let you know.

We compared notes on our day. She has three children
still home—ball practice, dinner, homework.
Our husbands need more T-shirts. I'll go to the
Leavenworth PX this weekend. Fort Riley was out last weekend.
Want to drive up with me?

Phone rang. Bob, the general, said it looked highly
unlikely the jeep was ours.
Unlikely enough I can call people back?
Yes, but don't be definitive. I won't; I know about that.
Yes, I'm sure you do, he smiled back.

Tucked into bed, the phone rang. Lynne and I reviewed the day:
Actions, thoughts and feelings as we relaxed into sleep
without our men next to us.

Hearing

The phone rings.
The voice,
belonging to the one I love so much,
is flat.
His attempts to sound normal
don't work.
He is depressed
Listen—
Hear the lack of cadence?
Tears
slow-cooked all day boil down my
cheeks as his confusion and pain
churn.
I want to hold him
in safe embrace.
I tell him but distance
intrudes.
I cannot wrap him in my arms.
I don't tell him I was sick
last night and this morning.
This phone call is not about me.

Terror on the Home Front

25 February 1991

Do you have the paper?
The one you were going to find Friday . . .
When my son called his teacher stupid.
Did you hear the news today?
    Long lines of prisoners.
Yes, and a Scud hit a hospital. Thanks.

Alone.

Two people of equal rank or higher come.
Get home.
No, she's wrong.
Call Lynne. No, I'll frighten her.
Get out of here. Go home.
I must be there when the officers come.
I'm remodeling the bathroom. I'll hire
someone to finish it in a day.
They don't come in an hour. Still,
go home. Wait alone.
When they come, call Onecia before they leave.
It's not true.
The Scud hit the other half of the hospital,
not the half he's in. He'll be home.
Look no one in the eye.
Get the plastic to recycle.

Pretend all is normal.
Buy gas because you won't want to afterward.
Gas before 4:00.

Scud hit Dhahran.
He's not there.

Recycle after 4:00.
I don't need to call my mother-in-law or son.
Throw the plastics in the bin.

The automatic door opened.
I walked onto the pavement.
The adrenaline in my veins and arteries
left.
All my blood dripped invisibly
from my fingertips and the soles of my feet.

A Letter and a Conversation

Letter, 1991:

Saudi Arabia is beautiful.
Its desert stretches horizon to horizon.
There are no mountains here and all
Nights are cool. I see a sky full of stars.
Reminds me of home
in the Oregon desert.

Conversation, 2013:

When Scuds came,
Everyone panicked, ran for their masks
and flak jackets. I didn't. Many cried.
I didn't.

"You had two tours under worse conditions,"
I said.

"Yeah," he replied as he put
another log on the fire.

Meeting Planes

I remember Robert being on the last of four flights home. He volunteered, not "army volunteered" but *really* offered, to take charge of the last detail. I met every plane coming home, thinking as chair of the family support group that I should in case some poor family was expecting their person to be on that plane and he or she wasn't, or someone was there and the family wasn't. Fortunately, those three flights went smoothly.

What did I do? Just tell the secretary of the school where I was principal that I was going out to meet another plane? Leave for a couple of hours and come back? That seemed weird. I must have, though, because planes did not come in half-day segments so I could take the morning or afternoon off.

Of course, I met the fourth plane, too. Very thoughtfully, and unexpectedly for me, about a half dozen of the other wives came to meet the last plane with the comment, "You were there for us. We're here for you." Wow, now there's a thanks.

Welcome Home

Onecia wept as I read my first letter
from you. "They're all the same. You
send him off. You'll welcome him home,"
said one Viet wife to another. Her husband
had fifty-four ambushes,
even more reconnaissance missions.
Who will welcome you home, Ed?
A drugstore in South Dakota that gives
free coffee and donuts to Vietnam vets—
twenty years late but better than never.

I take showers in my glasses and underwear
I brush my teeth wearing my hat, coat, and gloves
He's sixty miles away. What will I do when he goes?

You wore your two bars
I drove the '69 Camaro.
Your dog waits by the door
as Odysseus' dog waited for him.

I take showers in my glasses and underwear
I brush my teeth wearing my hat, coat, and gloves
He's sixty miles away. What will I do when he goes?

Early Sunday morning, the 410th left
flying in fishnets, silver anchovies
carried by helicopters as each two days
is three weeks long.

I take showers in my glasses and underwear
I brush my teeth wearing my hat, coat, and gloves
He's nine thousand miles away. I'll be fine when he comes home.

I met three planes. You were on the fourth.
Terri threw red, blue, and silver stars on us.
In the Viet Camaro we drove through cornfields,
burned forests, Badlands and Gallatin,
down the Columbia to the Pacific that is not
and into the sage. Butte had yellow ribbons
Corporal Nick Ouellette, Staff Sergeant Tom Kominski,
One on each light pole, a nation absolving its soul.

I took showers in my glasses and underwear
I brushed my teeth wearing my hat, coat, and gloves
This time we welcome you home from two wars.

Gold

He didn't know he should bring me a present. Nor did I. All I wanted was for him to come back alive and well.

Some people have a first and last name. Others have one name comprised of both. For this story it is Nancy Bond, who outranked him by one, but more important, she was good, efficient, and helpful. The conversation probably went like this.

"What have you bought Abigail?"

His blank stare followed by, "Nothing. I'm saving my money."

"Rob, we're going shopping when we get out of the desert."

"I don't know what she wants."

"Gold. She wants gold." Knowing he'd find someone to help or some work someone had neglected to do, Nancy Bond underlined this with, "I'll go with you."

Given that on our first Christmas he gave me a hairbrush and a pair of rubber boots, which I found unwrapped in the trunk of the car, a vial of sand would have astonished me. Across the years, flowers? He brought a bouquet twenty-one years earlier when our son was born. No, I didn't expect anything. I saw the cartouches some husbands had sent their wives, but knew better than to hope for anything like that. After all, officers and enlisted in his unit used to ask him when he last called home and inform him it was well passed time to call again.

Nancy Bond did well by me, but what is really important to me is that whenever I wear my gold camel, the small medallion, and earrings, I think of my husband and his tours. I think of all the other soldiers who have gone to war. I think of those currently serving in a war zone.

Because You Were
Never Thanked

I travel a lot from my home in Alaska. Seattle is my first stop to the Outside, a.k.a. the Lower 48. One day in the Seattle airport when getting my tea, I decided to buy a coffee card for the café's use to provide free coffee for those in uniform. I don't remember what year I started but it was around 2005. I will continue until all the troops are home from Iraq and now Afghanistan. I intended it to be an anonymous thank you, which it has been till now, a payback for the Vietnam veterans, including my husband, who were never thanked. I wanted to do my small part to thank those in uniform.

When my husband saw the charge on our card, he asked whom I took out for lunch at Dilettante Mocha Café for a hundred dollars. "Not lunch," I said, "it's an anonymous coffee for those in uniform."

"Thank you. That's very thoughtful," he said. He hasn't questioned these almost-monthly charges again.

I didn't expect to receive occasional notes from some troops. I thank the café and the managers, Liz then Mallory then Arielle, for helping me do this. A few months ago on one of my trips, I noticed that my card wasn't being used as much. I asked, hopefully, if there were fewer military people coming through. No, the TSA people are now donating their full coffee cards for the troops.

The note I received today, the first one I quote, made me decide not to remain anonymous. They each signed their last names; I removed them.

Thank you for the coffee! My husband was killed in Afghanistan in 2009 and I'm traveling to speak on his behalf. My free coffee was such a wonderful surprise. Thank you! Wife of Cpt. John H____.

Ma'am, It's people like you who make service members like myself even that much more prouder to serve. Thank you. SSG S___, U.S. Army

Thank you for the treat! :) SFC Michael B. F___, U.S. Army

Thank you so much for the coffee. It brightened my day as I fly home today to see my family for the first time in 9 months. It was very nice of you. God bless. PFC C___, Fort Lewis, WA

Thanks so much. People like you make this job worth doing. We strive to be worthy. Semper Fidelis, 1st LT William B___, 1st Battalion, 9th Marines.

Ma'am, Thank you very much for donating to Soldiers! Sgt. D___

Thank you so much for giving to the troops. I am going home on emergency leave and what you did and do for US soldiers has brightened my day and lifted my spirits. SPC L___

Most offer their thanks verbally, and I hear about those on my next trip through. Some of my favorites include the man who walked up and asked if the café gave a discount to people in uniform. The response he got was that they had one better for him—a free coffee. I feel guilty when the card goes down to zero and I've not flown for a while or I've forgotten that it's been over a month since I called to put more money on the card. I also remember the day I met the new manager and she thanked me quickly then said she couldn't say any more, or she'd cry. She turned and hurried to some task managers do.

One envelope was addressed to *Military Drink Card Lady*, another said *Military Gift Card Lady*.

How kind, I thought. *My good people, thank you for your service to your fellow citizens and for your notes. Providing a cup of coffee for you has been a simple pleasure for me.*

Another day I went to put more money on the card. The woman waiting on me said she was a veteran. I shook her hand and thanked her. She was tall and seemed quiet. I was about to ask her when and where she served when a young Asian woman rushed over. She thrust her hand to mine and said, "Thank you. Thank you." When I picked up my tea from her, she told me she was from Vietnam and wanted me to be sure to thank my husband. "Tell him thank you. Please thank him for me. Come visit. I go every year. I'll show you around. Come for our next Tet, our New Year celebration."

We will—if I can get my husband to take a vacation.

My Soldier

He walks through the garden, and his step has lost its hurry and bounce. His joy of life has dissipated as he grows older. He knows his limits and no longer uses his chain saw for three or four tanksful. He doesn't go for sixteen-mile hikes anymore, or even two-mile walks. He considers his work and walking around our forests exercise. He never complains.

I see the twenty-one-year-old man I met by literal accident a year after he returned from Vietnam. The young man jogging down the road in search of a phone, the handsome man with the gorgeous, broad smile that lights his face, the man I knew instantly I could sleep next to for the rest of my life. I hear the tenor voice with the sense of humor and fine wit, the one who asks piercing questions of life and people he knows. I still see the young and middle-aged man in and out of uniform.

He is my life partner even when he drinks too much, even when he loses his Irish temper for a minute or two then forgets why he was angry, because it's over. When he gives me an order, I salute him and laugh. He laughs, too. How did I know, when I fell in love with him the moment I met him, he would make such a good husband? He says he doesn't want to micromanage my life. Oh please do, and thank you for doing the dishes, grocery shopping, mowing, cutting and stacking the firewood, and all the other things you do.

He was a seventeen-year-old surgical tech. They waited until he turned eighteen before sending him to Vietnam. I told him I'd never met anyone before who had been there. He was astounded.

It's not always easy being married to a three-tour vet.

Eggshells

It's an old expression
—walking on eggshells.
Moments occur when
I tread so lightly
I do not break them.
Most of the time, though,
I walk at my normal pace of
four miles an hour.
Shells shatter with a high-
pitched, eardrum-piercing
screak—the sound of a
hydraulic motor gone wrong
while still moving all inner parts.
Or a bomb exploding.

From the neurons of a memory,
Triggered by a smell, a word,
a motion, perhaps something unseen
and unknown
synapses run at full throttle
to protect from harm in
war zones, but

There is no war at home.

Fixing the Problem

Perhaps it becomes the fabric of your soul
That much we know till
Some days we don't notice how you've morphed,
Developed silence.

It becomes part of you—the lines of age,
the wrinkles of disaster crease your soul.
Your cranium created new detours that
Weren't meant to become fixed highways.

For twenty years you walked through
muck as thick as La Brea Tar Pits—
dragging me along—
the one where so many saber-tooth
tigers died. It only took twelve years
of hard work to swim out the other side.
Covered with sand, scat, and bones, we took
Showers and washed each other's backs.

Perhaps now it has vaporized
Dissipated somewhere along the trail
Into air above Everest,
Sullied no one else's soul.

ē. Listen, America!

Shock and Awe

No, Mr. President. It's called
Damage and Destruction.
We families get
to live with it for the rest of our lives.

Support

*M*y husband enlisted the day after he graduated from high school. He was seventeen and a half. When he turned eighteen, he went to Vietnam for two tours. He got out of the army but signed up for the Army Reserves five years later—to have the money to buy a good Rototiller. Fast forward to Desert Storm when his unit was deployed. To welcome home and honor the troops from its various units, Topeka, Kansas, had a parade on Armed Forces Day, 1991. Marching in that parade, my husband felt welcomed home from Vietnam and the Gulf.

We are well educated and have good incomes and a good life. I always wanted to be my own person, never "the wife of." As I sat at my desk in 2010, it occurred to me that I *am* the wife of a soldier, and that will never change.

I don't know whether there should be a draft, but please, America, learn to recognize our military in their civilian clothing. Listen to the stories some will tell . . . and listen very carefully to the silence other veterans offer.

Until we all are a part of this support, we have no business sending people off to battle.

Listen

America: Learn to recognize them.

Listen to the stories some will tell.

Listen to the silence others offer.

If you can't hear them and weep in pain
Then never send them off to a war
that does not end when they come home.

Listen to the silence of dead voices,
to families that weep for generations,
to the raucous silence and unheard screams
veterans offer you.

Take One for Country

Stories hidden in daylight
Prowl from night shadows.

His wife holds her breath
As he mulls over desiccated days,

Releases the roil
that changed his innocent

selfless and gilded heart
to an aching, unquenchable grief.

He gave his soul to common good for a country
who does not care.

Lost Souls

*S*omewhere in the recent history of this country we have lost the souls of many of our military. In old Russia, a person was often referred to as a soul. A man owned not so many serfs, but so many souls. We have come to use that term when people die. Six souls were lost when *F/V Arctic Ranger* went down. Thirty-one souls were lost in Afghanistan in August 2011. Twenty-eight souls were lost in the Sandy Hook tragedy.

Since Vietnam, however, we have a new tragedy: the lost souls of too many who return from battle soul-wounded and wandering.

When I was four, I wore my red wool coat, hat, and leggings one winter day. I must have begged my father to let me sit by the door as he drove. As my father, his business friend, and I got into the car, I remember the two men joking about sitting close because I wanted the seat by the door. I remember being told to be careful of my hands when I closed the door. Oh yes, I assured him, knowing he had just spoiled me. My mother never would have let me sit on the outside. Carefully I leaned out, putting my left hand by the dashboard as I pulled the door closed with my right. Very methodically, I shut all my left fingers in the door. I'm sure I screamed, and the man next to me leaned to open the door immediately.

The closest hospital was Cushing Army Hospital. It was 1945. Imagine arriving at an army hospital with a crying little girl all dressed in red. I was hovered over by a half dozen men in pajamas and robes, and more stood in the background. The only man I'd even seen in pajamas was my father, and here I was looking at a hallway of pajamaed men. Some couldn't talk right. They all looked very ancient to me. Most likely they were younger than my forty-year-old father. My mother and aunt worked as Red Cross Gray Ladies there; now I got to see where they went each week. I was a novelty, a clean, well-dressed little girl with blonde curly hair who reminded them of their own daughters at home. All they wanted was to be close to the brightness of innocence, to wash away the horrors and nightmares of war. I think they comforted and charmed me out of my tears as my father and his friend faded into the background. Perhaps someone put some little bandages on my fingers, necessary for the tears but not the injury. When all was done, I wanted to tell my father we couldn't leave those men, I needed to stay there, continue to make them happier than they were when we walked in. At the age of four, of course, I made no such suggestion.

Lost souls. Souls lost somewhere on the battlefields of Europe and the Pacific waters. Souls lost in the fields of Vietnam and now in Iraq and Afghanistan. I hope we had fewer lost souls in World War II, because our nation supported that war. We did not support Vietnam or those sent there. Now our military is only 2 percent of the population, and most people don't know someone who has served. I thought I was brought up not knowing about war, but that is not true. Two cousins had husbands in World War II, and one of them died. I went to Cushing Hospital. We heard the war news on the radio every day as I, the youngest, sat curled in my father's lap. Boatloads of soldiers came into Boston Harbor during and after the war. How could I not know? How could I not feel empathy for those sad looking men?

We have lost souls wandering out of uniform. Those who are still healthy we hire and reward. The others we ignore.

Dear Mr. President

1 November 2009

Dear President Obama,

"The burden that both our troops and our families bear in any wartime situation is going to bear on how I see these conflicts," Mr. Obama said, speaking to reporters several hours later in the Oval Office. *"It is something that I think about each and every day."*

What do we bear?

Soldiers: Thoughts that never leave, emotions that linger even more than fifty years after World War II or forty-five years after Vietnam. Thoughts that wake them shaking and in a cold sweat. Coming home to sit on the edge of his bed, crying and shaking, day after day after day. A soldier coming home to screams: some his own and some those of his comrades.

Wives: Even after forty years we go on spousal alert. How's he going to react to this—gunfire in town or in our remote location, even out of hunting season? Someone yelling at him? Someone accidentally bumping into him at the mall? Being seated at the table in a restaurant with his back to the room, the window, or the entrance? My accidentally dropping a dish or pan in the kitchen? A child's balloon popping behind him? How will he behave the next time we argue?

A parent of two of my elementary school students is crippled with PTSD. He's a Vietnam veteran, so damaged he doesn't remember his enlistment, shipment, location, or discharge dates. He can't apply for benefits without those dates, and the local VA has offered no help to locate his files. One day he showed up at school with a bathrobe tie holding up his pants. Another day he had a flashback in my office.

What is the cost? I talked to a friend one afternoon when he was home on two-week leave from Iraq. He interspersed our casual conversations about how good it was to be home and how good it was to see me with one sentence repeated about a half dozen times—"I killed a twelve-year-old boy." I wanted to put my arms around this over-six-foot man as I stood on the road and he sat in the driver's seat of the borrowed car. Just trying to absorb that reality, aren't you? He was nineteen then. I know enough to know he'll take that unresolved issue to the grave with him.

What is the cost? My sister-in-law made a casual comment on the phone—how different her brother was when he came back. I was taken aback. I met him the year after he came home. How come no one ever told me before? What did you mean by that? I never saw my husband gung ho about anything. Driven, oh yes, oh so driven. It never mattered whether he was bucking hay bales, slinging green chain, putting a log on his sawmill, or being a patient and fun-loving nurse, he is driven to do his best. But gung ho, no. My heart aches to know the man I fell in love with the moment I saw him, the guy who didn't tell me his name but called me the next day to say he'd fallen in love with me. Lovely, kind, and handsome, but I missed the gung ho part. Years later, as we walked across Fort Riley one day in the late 1980s, we passed a group of soldiers playing volleyball. "That reminds me of when we played volleyball in between surgeries in the Mekong Delta." And on the story went.

"You never told me that before," I replied.

"I told you all about Vietnam."

Maybe you thought and felt about it in my presence, but for three decades you rarely talked about it.

And he's one of the healthy ones.

We don't need more veterans. Too many of them and their families bear a very heavy burden. We need to take care of them first.

I was chairperson of the family support group for my husband's four-hundred-member 410th Army Evacuation Hospital when they went to Desert Storm. I came home from my day as principal of an elementary school to spend the next seven hours on the phone with wives, mothers, girlfriends, and husbands of the unit's members. As a professional, I have written a handbook for people with PTSD, which will be published soon. Some of my writings about soldiers have been published.

I am aware that you have far more information than I on which to base your decision to send more troops to Afghanistan, but your statement helped me clarify my thoughts and feelings on more troops going off to war. Their families need them here.

With respect for you and your office,

Abigail B. Calkin, PhD

Goodbye

When the troops went off to Iraq,
our hearts filled with thoughts of farewells.
We treasured our nugget of love even more,
nurtured it, held it, examined it,
kept it in the woven basket by the bed,
sang Hallelujahs to the embrace of sleep,
Ave Marias to the morning light as younger
wives, husbands, parents, and children
smiled as if all were well.

vi. Recovery

Platoon

"No, you may not go see *Platoon* with me. I'm going alone." He was right. I would have been watching him, not the movie.

A day or two later, our son and I went. On the drive home in the 1969 red 350 Rally Sport Camaro, he said, "Dad was only six months older than I when he went, and I'm just a kid."

"And I'm driving the car he spent every penny of his Vietnam money on."

We walked into the house at suppertime. Perhaps Robert had fixed dinner while we were gone. I'm married to a man who eats and leaves the table, a product of a ranching family and a father who was sheriff—no idle chatter. This evening, though, we sat at the table while he told us stories—his good sergeant, his bad sergeant, the Highlands, the Delta, different surgeries, the crush of wounded as helicopter after helicopter came in. All stories and names I had not heard. I don't remember all his stories. I just remember he sat and talked for three hours. As priests listen to confessions, we sat silently as he poured his soul into our empty water glasses and dinner plates.

He did not mention my favorite one. He had eight hours off before returning to the OR. He went for a walk and laid down at the edge of the jungle. A spider was on a leaf or limb. She descended to his nose, then scurried back up her line, an anchor for her web. He spent the eight hours lying there, watching the spider weave her web.

Where Did You Leave

Where did you leave parts of yourself—
with the spider or vines in the jungle,
on the streets of Saigon,
in the Montagnard hills,
in the desert under stars,
with some of the patients who survived
or did not?

Change

You enlisted as a private, retired as a major,
but the USA didn't want you to remember
what changed you.
Now you've forgotten—
not deep inside your war-laden neurons
but in your daily life.

How much does it take not to remember those moments?

The Quaker and the Sergeant

I was raised a gentle life
Knew not a soldier till I met my own.
Stood before his conflicted, raging soul.
Naked and sweetly unaware,
He calmed against my skin.

Korean War Memorial

*L*incoln was seven when his father, Larry, the captain of a commercial fishing boat, had an accident in which his deckhand was killed. The accident put Larry near death and then disabled for life. Years later, on a trip together to Washington, DC, Larry and Lincoln went to the Korean War Memorial. Larry was three years old when his father, Leslie Hills, was killed in Korea in 1951, south of Koesan where his outfit was guarding a mountain pass. The memorial consists of a company of soldiers, such as Larry's father might have led, crossing a rice paddy. The day they went there, the scene was made all the more real as rain pelted down on solid soldiers in their capes and gear, now literally in a field of water . . . statues in a rice paddy viewed by the son and grandson of a first lieutenant killed in Korea.

One of my screensavers is a winter photograph of the silent troops thigh-deep in snow. I picture Larry's father there, this man who had been at Angaur, Peleliu, Guadalcanal, Negarigo, New Caledonia, and Leyte before going to Japan for the occupation. After World War II, he was placed on inactive army reserve duty, meaning they could call him up if they needed him. He was recalled to active duty in 1950 with orders for Korea.

The captain of a boat is responsible for all lives on board. The lieutenant is responsible for the lives of his men. In my book *The Night Orion Fell*, I tell the story of Larry's father:

> How many lives had Leslie Hills been responsible for? What were his feelings when one of his men was killed? I called Larry one day while writing the book to tell him I had created a conversation between him and his long-deceased father. Was it close to accurate? Larry was silent before he softly said he has had such conversations

with his father while driving, hiking, falling asleep. He now knows he has a permanent identification with him: the feeling of responsibility for a life not saved. But this one person he could talk to, the most important person who could understand, is not available to exchange the few sentences that would acknowledge their shared personal grief and level, at least for the moment, the density of that feeling.

Not Alone

Humpty Dumpty
struggles to patch cleaved pieces.
Instead he terrifies children,
blanches mica wives
as his broken eggshell
defies full stitchery.

Jagged Edges

How do you put the pieces together?
Asked the young enlisted wife.
I never did, but I learned
How to maneuver jagged edges,
Answered the officer's wife.

Dogs and Cats

*A*bout to deploy, we lay in bed watching the sunset. The dog sat at the side of the bed, the cat lay on his chest. He patted them both.

"I'm really going to miss Willoughby and Phantom." And he continued to stroke them both.

I lay there silently . . . waiting . . .

"What about me?" I mocked myself.

Somewhat surprised to hear a voice in bed with him, he looked at me. "Oh, I'll miss you too."

Years later in Alaska, we had to put Phantom down. I held the dead cat in a box on my lap; Robert drove the deserted road and bawled on the way home.

"He was my best friend. I used to tell him everything."

I wondered what tales of my transgressions that cat heard, but I was also glad my husband had someone to talk to. We buried him in the forest in front of the house.

Ten years later, when one of our dogs was old and dying, Robert spent two nights sleeping in the pickup with the dog. The next morning he said he was too stiff and couldn't do that another night. He called a friend who shot the dog, and Robert buried him by the sawmill.

Two years later, he spent nights with Homer, who was dying of old age. He took his sleeping bag to the woodshed and stretched it out alongside Homer on the cold October Alaska nights. At least they were out of the rain. Once again, he called his friend to come shoot the dog.

Both these times I was out of town, and as I sat in the car at the Little Bighorn Battlefield, I heard my husband's sobs and felt grateful he had these animals who where such good friends, whom he could spoil, friends he would tell anything to that he was not able to tell me. Sometimes I wish he could talk to me more, even though I realize that he has nonjudgmental and loving companions to share his moments of woe with. I am loving but not always nonjudgmental.

Temper

No behavior has one source. My husband's temper comes from many— not exclusive but many—sources. He grew up with a crazy mother in an Irish household and community. He went from there to Vietnam and two years in an army surgical hospital right behind the front lines. Some days he worked the full twenty-four hours or more with no break, one time thirty-seven hours straight in surgery as they all tried to save lives. Some days, privates up to doctors and support to surgical staff ran out to meet the helicopters as they brought in too many wounded and dying.

Fifteen years later, when our son was almost a teenager, my teenage niece came to live with us for high school. One day, when she was furious at I do not know what, she stood a foot away, screaming at me. My body was tense, breath held, shoulders slightly up, fists clenched, all in a contrary effort to relieve my stress. Suddenly, she yelled in a continuous staccato, "And furthermore I'm not mad at you I'm mad at me but since I can't yell at me I'm going to yell at you!"

I breathed; my shoulders went down, my hands unclenched. No, the person who yells is not angry with the audience. But when was the last time you tried to yell at yourself? I tried once, in front of a mirror. I laughed. Had to. I looked so ridiculous, my face contorted, my eyes piercing.

I won't claim Robert and I never argue and yell absurd things at one another. I will say though, that when he, or anyone is angry, I'm much more able to listen, to hear what he's angry about, and now know I am almost never the recipient. I hear the angry words and, since they don't belong to me, I can listen.

I used to be a principal and had an angry mother come to yell at me. I said nothing. At the end of about ten minutes, she said, "Thank you for listening to me. Now can we talk about what I came to talk to you about?" All because I said nothing.

So when my husband yells, I listen—and in about ten minutes, we talk.

Pieces

*Y*ou tell me in pieces between lighting the fire and sitting to drink your coffee, or between putting on your coveralls and going outside to shovel snow, or between your shower and going to work in the garden. I listen carefully to sentences and vignettes as I try to comprehend what went on outside and in. Some stories are funny or poignant, like the officer who refused to set up his tent. So you, a captain, were doing it for him. Major Crisler came along, asked you what you were doing. Major So-and-So refuses to set up his tent, you said. Crisler stopped to help. He respected you for doing it; you thought he was great for helping. You both thought the indolent major was a jerk but never made that comment, just that glance of agreement. Other stories were matter of fact. The Iraqis were firing Scuds and you walked around doing your job while others ran for their helmets, masks, and flak jackets; some were even crying. I can feel your thought—this is so much easier than Vietnam. Or when you told me just the other day about driving a transport truck, perhaps a deuce and a half, from Pleiku to An Khe to Quy Nho'n and back a few times. There was pride in your voice and you straightened to attention.

I try to piece together stories of jungle, desert, delta, and return—the uniformed pieces of you. I've heard your worries, watched your face dissolve to distress in the days before you boarded the bus for your deployment to Desert Storm, seen the anger and tears when you're home, all which you deny in days or years to come. You've forgotten them just like the keys or credit card you lose—too many pockets, you say. I think too many stories and feelings are tucked away in hidden pockets, and that's okay, because

I have my own hidden pockets, too. I try to piece yours together to understand more the man I love and married. All I come up with is that you are so good for me—you make it possible for me to get up and just say good morning. How can I feel depressed when I see your smile and laughing eyes, when your pragmatism reminds me the landfill is open today, or that we're walking out to a friend's house for the afternoon? The world goes on, and you make sure I put one foot in front of the other. You are my third prong on the plug.

As we walked the dog one afternoon in the '80s on the grounds of Topeka State Hospital, you said you figured you had PTSD. Then, a few years ago in a phone call, you told me something that happened and your reaction of overwhelming fury, clearly stating you have PTSD. In your soft voice you've mentioned it several times in the past months. What brings it to the fore now? You remind me of Grandfather Barry who let his feelings lie dormant for fifty years before he told his daughter to go see his old comrade from County Cork, Dave York.

I listen. I care. I hold the words and stories you tell me in my thoughts and feelings. I write only some of them.

How can you be so pragmatic and yet so complicated? Me? I'm just complex all the time.

Flash of Light

We live in a small, nine-hundred-square-foot house in the middle of a forest. Our kitchen appears big because it has five windows and two doors, but the floor space is ten feet by ten feet.

My husband and I stood at the stove as I checked the homemade noodles and he tended the stir-fry of smoked black cod and vegetables. It was late fall, and we'd already had a few feet of snow. Suddenly, the deep new snow silently fell off the roof, reflecting the kitchen lights as it went down. It would land with a thud, but not before Robert responded to what he saw. He startled.

"Wow," he said. "I thought that was the flash that you see right before a bomb goes off." He paused then turned to me and said with that twinkle in his eyes, "Now I don't want you to think I have PTSD because of that."

I teased, "Whatever would make me think that?" We bumped hips with a grin and leaned into one another as we put the finishing touches on dinner.

It's been forty-three years since Viet Cong bombs exploded around him. Left alone and not reconditioned, Pavlovian conditioning hangs around for a long time . . . a lifetime. I hadn't noticed any flash. Nor did I know till then that there was a flash of light a fraction of a second before a bomb explodes.

Vietnam—Then and Now

A neighbor phoned when he returned from four months in Southeast Asia. He kayaked in Vietnam's Gulf of Tonkin in water filthy with plastic, tires, shoes, and other debris. He put his sandals outside his door at night because no one wears outside shoes in the house. They were gone the next morning. After we hung up, I told Robert what he said.

"I lost a *hell of a lot* more than that over there. A pair of sandals. What's he worried about? Yeah, Carlos, a pair of sandals. I lost my virginity over there!" He started to laugh.

"I'm going to tell him he only stayed two and a half weeks and he got to leave. I spent two years over there and *couldn't* leave. Wait till he comes over and I talk to him," he said with an Irish twinkle in his blue eyes as we walked to the living room.

We sat on the sofa facing one another, our legs outstretched and touching. Conversation, mixed with both gentle and side-holding laughter, rambled on about Vietnam, war, and the army. Twenty minutes later, we both had tears in our eyes. The laughter ended and the tears dried as we finished sharing one more moment of release.

The Second Wall

A wall holds you,
keeps you in one piece
for others to see—

until the day our two-year-old
grandson said
"I love you Grandpa Goose."

You wept at his
unconditional
love.

vii. Resolution, Always Partial

Biography

17
Boot camp,
medical training, Brooks Army Hospital 1966

18
1967 Quy Nho'n, Pleiku, Dong Tam,
Lai Khe, Bien Hoa, Lon Binh 1969

24
married, one son

42
Desert Storm 1991

66
Alaska, same
woman 2015

Universality

It's larger than our marriage
larger than the sum of us.
The universe walks into our room,
Lies down on the bed—
Takes form as
mastodon, whale or planet,
wraps around the in and out of us,
never leaves.
Curls in the corner and naps
as we walk our daily lives.

Protocol in Bed

Soon to fall asleep again
I said Lovely. Thanks.
He replied Yes Ma'am.

Yes Ma'am. In bed.
To his wife.
A second of silence and I
burst out laughing. So did he
till we cuddled to sleep.
Protocol!
It never evaporates.

Smell of Death

Some yellow-lit mornings
I pass out at the kitchen sink,
come to on the dining room rug
or living room sofa.

Or perhaps it's a moonless winter.
I'm lying nude on the ceramic
bathroom floor calling for help.
I thought I was dying

He continues eating supper, washing
dishes, or says he thought I was
bleeding, and stumbles
sleepily back to bed.
I am always reassured:

I do not smell like death.
If I did, he would act
as he did at war,
Try to save my life.

Gratitude

I am grateful:
My husband is alive, home with me.
We are grateful he retired
before this last round of wars.
He did his three tours.
He does not belong to the Army
anymore.

Exile

After the war is over
After he is home
The battles continue—
Orders, distance, alcohol
Occasional thousand-yard stares—
What else resides in there?
Anger? Depression? Love?

I hold my arms open for the
Sweet man I kissed goodbye.

Dead Reckoning

I'm not some dead guy
on an OR table.
Don't shut your emotions from me.
Don't slam the door
or zip up the bag.

Hold Me Close No Matter the Distance

Hold me close with your smile,
witty comments and lovemaking
—all the touch of a rose petal against my skin—
your laughter that sparkles your eyes as it
turns my serious moments into daily reality.
Hold me close with all the things you do
for me—dishes, vacuuming, wood for the stove
you cut, stack and put in the wood box,
grocery shopping, heavy work in the garden.
In sleep at night or naps
you curl me
in the sound of your voice and pragmatic words.
I'll make you a sign that says
A man's work is never done.
Hold me close as I spot you walk through the woods,
a Magritte painting as you move amidst the trees.
Hold me as we take two- or fifteen-mile walks,
go out in the skiff together or when you boat alone.
Then I miss your clothes and skin,
your hair and varied smells. Then I worry till
I welcome you home again.
Today you smelled like gasoline from the sawmill.
When I miss your presence,
I see your face.
Your eyes and smile envelop me.
I see the handsome man in uniform

—military, nursing, or coveralls—
All of you holds me close no matter the distance.
I married the right man.
How can I ever miss you for you
Are always here with me.

Any Wife

Even after 40 years I go on spousal alert:
How's he going to react to
Helicopters or gunfire in our neighborhood,
Someone yelling at him,
Someone bumping into him at the mall,
Being seated at a table in a restaurant if his back isn't to the wall,
A grandchild's balloon accidentally bursting nearby,
Me dropping a dish or pan in the kitchen,
Or walking up behind him?

Uniforms

*F*our years after we met, I saw my husband in uniform for the first time. What was my reaction? I took new notice of how handsome he looked. Something about a man in uniform . . . What was my previous contact with uniforms? My cousin's husband, Robert, showed up at our house in his navy whites during World War II. I was three or four years old and answered the door. He stood on the other side of the screen a step down from the front hallway of the house. This made me about eight inches taller than I was, so I had a different look at him, almost seemed his equal, although he had a daughter my age. He seemed a vision of loveliness when he came off the sea to get a taste of home. My mother was the eldest of six, and we lived in a big house in a suburb of Boston that was sanctuary for family and friends to visit or live at times of connubial death or war. Robert was the first one to come in uniform, perhaps the only one. Other than that, my experience with uniforms was looking at the pictures in *Life* during the war and seeing sailors and soldiers coming to Greenwich Village on leave when we lived there during the Korean Conflict.

My parents had saved all *Life* magazines since the first issue in the mid-'30s. They were stored on the steps of the closed stairway that led from the garden-level kitchen to the first-floor dining room. When my parents bought the house, they closed that stairway off and put a kitchen on the first floor. A part of my childhood was going to that darkened stairwell, leaving the door open into the sunroom and looking at pictures in the old issues. It was a big and busy house with lots of people living there, anywhere from six to eleven of us. Censorship of reading did not exist in that household.

Why was my father not in uniform? Coming from a seafaring family, he wanted to join the navy. When Pearl Harbor was bombed, he was thirty-seven, married with four children, and, for some reason in those days, needed his wife's written permission to join. He did not pass the physical because he was colorblind. Too old to be drafted into the US Army or Marines, that was the end of his military options.

It was strange for me to find myself as an adult living with a man who put on a uniform even one weekend a month. The Vietnam War had just ended and he had his Rototiller. I confess, I didn't know how to respond to his re-upping so I pretty much ignored it and was not a part of it. But as our marriage was and would continue to be, it was important for him to participate in the reserves. I was not a part of that decision making and would just live with it. The only time I put my foot down was when we lived in Topeka and he wanted to buy a handgun for protection. I told him the day he brought a gun into the house was the day I moved out.

Don't get me wrong. When I was a teenager, I had friends with rifles and handguns, and we'd go out in the country and target shoot. I was a good shot and loved doing that. I even had the opportunity to shoot the pistol a friend's great-grandfather had carried in the Civil War. He had to pour the bullets for it himself. "It's not accurate. Aim low and to the left," he told us.

By the time it was my turn, I'd forgotten the instruction and aimed directly at the target. Hit it dead on.

"How you'd do that?" he hollered.

"I aimed at it."

His ancestor's pistol was still accurate. Living in remote Alaska now, I own a hunting rifle if I choose to hunt. I occasionally fish instead and like that immensely.

When I became chair of the family support group for the 410th Evacuation Hospital, I was suddenly thrown into the world of uniforms. I loved Robert. There was no way I was not going to offer my full and unqualified support for him and his comrades. At that point I became an army wife.

For sixteen years I had ignored that I was married to a veteran and member of the military. I ignored it because I lacked comprehension.

Ten years ago, I began to write *The Night Orion Fell*, a book about a commercial fishing accident that involved a Coast Guard rescue. Robert's caution to me as I was about to leave for parts of Alaska, Washington, and Oregon on a series of interviews of these rescuers was, "Behave yourself." *Behave myself?* What did he think I would do? I finally figured out that he meant for me to behave as an officer's wife. That's easy; my mother raised me to be dignified. I can do that.

Something else happened as I wrote that book. Several people here in Alaska suggested I join the Coast Guard Auxiliary. I liked that idea because the Coast Guard's work along our shores is vital to our very lives. I liked it until I was promoting the book at the Working Waterfront Festival in New Bedford. I stopped by the booth the Auxiliary had and realized they were all in uniform. I shrank inside realizing I could not get a military uniform on. I could picture holding the pants to put my leg inside, maybe even get my foot off the floor, but I could not get my foot past the waistband.

It makes no sense that I can love my man in his uniform, admire others who wear the uniform, help them out, but no matter how I try to think about it, I could not join any aspect of the military other than being the wife of, a role I wear proudly.

Marriage

Ebb tides take plights out.
Flood tides fill a life's moments
beneath moon and sun.

Life is not perfect
but, amidst open seas, well
negotiated.

What He Learned

This morning sun shines on new snow.
Yesterday he said what he learned
in Vietnam
made him a fuller person.
He took a desert's small town vision, turned
it broader—saw
another religion, way of life, and
lush jungle. He
questioned himself, goals that now
lay jumbled—was America the greatest,
how gung ho was he?

After Vietnam, he came home,
confronted some of war's demons,
altered everyday life.
Ambled about, fell in love, became a father,
a nurse, and a man weighed by duty. Just now,
he stopped at the coffee shop to explain he
waited twenty minutes, lost his patience,
didn't mail my package. Weighed by duty,
he could not wait till I came home an hour later.
I was in the midst of reading this,
when he entered
on cue.

This morning sun shines on new snow.

Diaspora

Why do the nations rage so furiously together?
—*Psalms*, 11.1.2. In Handel's *The Messiah*.

Diaspora: dispersion, scattering, coming from a Greek word meaning "to sow." Originally applied to Jewish people who were dispersed from their homeland, it is also applied to other groups—the diaspora of white Russians fleeing their homeland, the diaspora of African Americans to northern US cities, the diaspora of Hispanics from Mexico to the States, the diaspora of Native Americans. I also think about the diaspora of soldiers. They are trained, sent off as units in World War II, as individuals to Vietnam, as units to Iraq and Afghanistan. From World War II they came home by boat, a week or two of forced togetherness, a chance to weep, to talk, to hope for the idyllic home they left behind. From Vietnam, Iraq, and Afghanistan, they arrive by plane. They sleep, or sit with the thousand-yard stare. Before they realize their surroundings and can talk with their buddies, the plane lands. They have mere hours to change from battlefield to billboards, city noise, and hundreds of people in a mall.

When I leave my home in Alaska—off the road system, remote, four hundred people—and go to New Orleans or New York, Lima or London, I am lost. I don't speak the language of these scurrying, preoccupied people. I feel confused, defensive, and have a wish for everyone to evaporate.

I revert to old habits developed from living in New York City or London. I pause to view store windows to see who may be behind me; I don't give a hoot what the store is displaying. Looking can pass as normal. Only if I flatten myself against the window or a wall and don't move, only if I refuse to leave my apartment or house, am I outside the frame that would make someone take notice. I can roil inside, but if it leaks out before I calm the oceans, it is a problem.

If I feel disconnected in my own country, what must soldiers feel when they come home? Occasionally, when I look at or listen to my husband, I see a man who was at war. Most times I see someone as normal as the rest of us. I see someone who wouldn't qualify for a PTSD label. But still . . . there are those worst moments that let me know I married a veteran.

When I look at veterans, I see a scatter, a disconnect. It's as if there are parts of a skeleton that needs reassembling. It's not a foot here or a femur there, but the hand of an emotion, an eyebrow tormented by anger. I can't see what courses through my husband's feelings when I walk up behind him and he jumps and snaps at me. I often see it in the morning as he sits in the rocking chair, staring out the window while sipping his coffee, his dog or cat by him. Most web their way through that veil and heal themselves. Some, though, are scattered, dispersed within themselves—a diaspora. Somehow, they need to re-sow the seeds of their emotions and thoughts, grow new roots, sprout new plants, and heal the connection from the intensity of battle to the calmness of today.

The Wall

The wall teems with life. People walk
reflections in color
against line after line of names
Ulysses Battle, +John M. Brucher, Rodney M. Chapman,
Virgil C. Combs, John P. Cook, Gerald A. Gray, . . .
I want to be alone
to respect the names of those who died
in field, en route, in hospital,
in mud of delta, in jungles of the Highlands
under hands of doctors of twenty-eight,
nurses twenty-two and surgical techs in their teens
or surgeons who triaged on the floor in the corner
while others saved someone else's son.
Your name is not there
and that has made all the difference in my life.
Last year Emmanuel, a taxi driver, took
me to The Wall. Go, go see your husband's friends.
I left everything on the seat.
Ran past the walk turned to blurt a cry of tears
as the black granite *V* cut the gut of ground,
caught my eye, and punched my lungs.
I tipped him all I had, $8 for a $12 fare.
I'd have tipped him $50 if I'd had it.
Today my husband lives
and nameless, countless others too.
I know no name on that Wall but they are
husbands, fathers, brothers, sons,
comrades-in-arms.

194

In that black granite gut of a *V*, also lies
my husband's innocence and that of his comrades.

James Carlson, Layne Clifton, James L. Hull, Paul Sheer . . .

Silence

We have entered the silence, not the silence of unspoken anger but of resolution, of peace. Most of the time he has reached a truce with himself, a truce for us. Mostly gone are the temper tantrums, the frequent outbursts that let me know I had married a man from an Irish family. I realized later it was as much or more related to his two years in Vietnam. Twenty-two months, he always says.

We have entered the negotiated realm where we know what sets the other on the edge of the knife's blade. I work hard, very hard, to be punctual. I am no longer hours late. He has learned not to explode if I'm only fifteen minutes late. Most of the time.

We live in the silence of Alaska. Go for walks together or alone. We can fall asleep without talking, but often wake at 1:00 a.m. to talk for an hour or two about the meaning of life, a political event, or thoughts I had walking at the beach and he had while bucking up a standing dead pine for the woodstove, then spoon or make love to sleep till the morning. We still think our private thoughts that may or may not become public and are at peace with that. At least I think we're at peace.

No More MREs

He brought them home from field maneuvers
Stored them in the floor-to-ceiling cabinet behind the kitchen stove.
We rummaged through them in preparation for family
camping trips. Ate them.
On a very lazy evening when no one wanted to cook
and there were no leftovers, we'd go to the
cupboard and haul out dinner, sit in the living
room by the fire and eat MREs.
Yesterday I thought
He's been out so long we don't have any more MREs.
I miss that plain dark green wrapper with black letters.
Today's camp food with its colorful packet that entices one
to eat is not the same.
All the MRE says is
Eat.

Retirement

Basic and special training at 17
Retired at 52.
Lost his military family.

No thanks after Vietnam,
Today every retirement check is the
Army's personal thank you.

Veterans Day 2012

The best part of his
Veterans Day was in prison
When he passed out meds.
Two inmates saluted him.
One gave the slow salute used at funerals,
The other attempted a correct one.
Still, their honor stirred him.

Retirement Papers

We spent the last few days filling out his retirement papers. As we drove to get a cup of hot chocolate, Excursion Ridge loomed in the clear October air. Still without termination dust, blueberry bushes with their bark exposed to the world, made the tops of the high hillsides glow a deep, rich red.

"I'll never know all the issues Vietnam brought up for me. I'll live with them unresolved." I studied his face as he spoke then turned away to distract myself, keep my tears from brimming over. Two consecutive tours, twenty-two months in country, and thirty-eight years later he says this. Thus his delay in filling out retirement papers until I nudged him to sit down and finish what I had almost completed for him. Once they were faxed to Fort Richardson for a final check before he mailed them, he thanked me saying he'd never have done it if I hadn't pushed him.

I was raised a Quaker in a family that knew war was sometimes reality. Being married to a Vietnam vet was okay because once home he was privately against that war and happy to be out of the military. Skip to five years later when he wanted a Rototiller but couldn't afford it.

He came home one Thursday to announce, "I just re-upped."

"Just now?"

"Yes. On my way home from the hardware store. In the reserves. I'm still a sergeant and my pay is fifty dollars a month. We can buy the Rototiller."

I was supposed to be happy about this. I wasn't. He did buy a very good Rototiller, though. Some sort of a double-bladed one, two gears, four horsepower.

Skip seven years. He used his GI bill to go to nursing school. With that college degree, he automatically became a second lieutenant. Only it wasn't automatic. He had the common enlisted resentment of officers and didn't want to be "one of them." He delayed until he was told to fill out the promotion papers or get out. He followed orders.

Skip ten years. Now a captain, his unit was activated for Desert Storm.

I continued to work full-time as a principal. Chaired the family support group for these four hundred soldiers. Took a shower in my underwear and glasses. Brushed my teeth one winter day in my hat, coat, and gloves. So preoccupied, I couldn't even laugh at myself.

I managed everything, including about seven hours every day after work with phone calls from and to various families. My support was two to four daily phone calls with my crazy mother-in-law. My writer friends kept me glued together in our Wednesday evening meetings. Lynne, another officer's wife, and I ended each day with a 2300 phone call just to be able to get to sleep. Her husband had been on his way to Vietnam when the conflict ended. Lucky them.

Managed everything except trying to redo one of the bathrooms in our seventy-five-year-old home. I called a friend as I sat on the floor of the bathroom one Saturday morning, crying when I realized I couldn't scrape and paint it in one day. I blathered on till he ordered, "Shut up!" in his Vietnam-sergeant style. I shut up. "I'll be there in five minutes. Be ready." I didn't ask for what. I got dressed. The hell with breakfast or tea. He drove to a lake out in the country where we went for a walk. Talked about fishing and eagles, hawks and poetry. Probably talked about war, too.

Managed everything except when my husband told me he'd volunteered, not "army volunteered" but really offered, to stay behind with the last detachment of mostly enlisted. Packed up the last of the field unit. Washed every speck of sand off all parts of all the trucks. I was livid and made the unforgivable mistake of writing him an angry letter telling him how I felt. That's a bad thing to do. My unspoken orders were that I stay home, be supportive, put up with whatever, and never say anything wrong. I flunked being a good wife. I hope he'll forgive me when I get over being embarrassed about that and apologize to him.

Yes, I apologized just the other day, but that kind man readily forgave me saying he knew being a wife at home was hard, too.

Why He Is Who
He Is

1.

As he packed his duffle bags
I smelled the thick odor of canvas,
odor of Einstein's
Army Surplus store.

When he returned,
They smelled of dry sand
stuck in every stitch of canvas.

Twenty years later he uses one every week
as he flies back and forth to Juneau.
On the faded bottom
his rank, name, and SSN barely
recognizable even to the two of us.

2.

He has calmed.
Does not yell so much.
Still doesn't like sudden change,
especially from the rear.

"I'll get another check this week."
Thanks it says. Thanks for three tours.

Thanks for 28 years
years that changed your life for the better
years that make your soul ache unpredictably.

3.

I don't know where Uncle Joe's leather helmet went.
Did you give it to Seth or Abi, Barry or Phil?
The one he wore as a WWII pilot.

I hear your stories
Green canvas, uniforms, patches, blood,
four rows of ribbons,
dead bodies,
blown out of bed, helicopters,
boots, perfection, 18 years old,
Jim Carlson, Lon Binh, Pleiku,
Bedouins, reconstructing a face,
sadness, hugs, tears, drained the life

4.

I stroke his hand, each finger
wide from his work at the chainsaw or sawmill,
his 41 zigzag stitches lost in swollen flesh.
When he returned from the desert
delicate stitching of others' surgeries reduced
his own swelling and I could stroke
his jagged, chainsawed scar again.

Taps

*T*he day of my father-in-law's funeral, Robbie's cousin, Ernie, told us that in Irish Catholic tradition, he stayed up all night with George at the funeral home. It didn't matter that George was not Catholic. He had married into the Barry family and tradition had to be followed. This is how Ernie showed his respect and honor to George, tradition, and family. Robbie had been home from Vietnam for four years and had not yet re-upped into the Army Reserves. He had, however, cut his long hair to a standard haircut his father would have appreciated. Someone commented it was too bad George had not seen it before he died. To that, Robert said, "No. It's good enough I cut my hair."

Once he came to the fork in the road, chose to enlist, and then wrote Vietnam as his first choice for location, there was no turning back. Without realizing its impact on the rest of his life, he chose his path.

From my perspective as a school psychologist and a behaviorist who analyzes people's behavior, thoughts, and feelings, I have studied the number of reasons people do things and everyone gives a number between twenty-five and fifty. I have reviewed how we develop attitudes. One researcher found ninety-eight elements form attitudes. That means I may have fifty reasons why I smiled or yelled at my husband and ninety-eight elements that influenced why I married him. No wonder it is so hard for me to figure out myself. No wonder I sometimes simply say that I'm not going to figure out something. How do I resolve that an intelligent and well-educated person sometimes sees auras and senses things before they happen? I don't know, but I now assume it came from looking death in the eye when I was five. It's not an experience I can forget. How do I resolve that a Quaker married a sergeant? That one should be easier to figure out. I decided not to bother for it was too complex and less important than dying. What difference does it make that I'm a Quaker anyway? I love him. I married him decades ago and even though "till death do us part" wasn't in our vows, we behave and honor our marriage and partnership as if it were.

Where does the strength to make it through life's difficult moments come from? Are we taught as children? Does it come from the attitudes we develop? A statement a person made to us on a bus or at a family gathering? I have no need to know a right answer. I don't know how Robert honors the lives he saw lost. I don't know how he washes the aura of death from his hands. I know, though, that it must be difficult for him to wrestle with that amorphous force that took over his life. Where does he get the strength to get through all this? Are there cue cards for emotions? I don't know, but I know his drive, his caring about people, his humor about the small things in life, his kind eyes and manner, and his living in the present continue to keep him moving forward. I don't know how much laughing he and I do, but I know he's great at one-liners, playing with words, and bringing a smile to my face.

I also know each of us can celebrate and honor those who served. We can play taps for those who died. We can play taps for those who lost a part of their soul. We can take that extra step to make the world a better place, to help fill the empty spot someone else no longer can. We can relearn how to smile with joy, at least occasionally, as we did when we were five.

Welcome
Home

My Thanks

I am deeply indebted to my husband who has shared two-thirds of his life and so much of his soul with me. He's told many stories. I do not pretend I have told them accurately. Instead, I tell them from my best recollections and from the impressions they made on me. This book also contains stories I heard from other soldiers that touched me deeply. Being married to a soldier made me sensitive to the stories they tell. None of the men or women meant to tell me a story—they were just sharing the ache in their gut. I remain appreciative of the trust they placed in me when they shared parts of their lives.

My husband has not read these and offered insights. He turns away from them, even from those about others, because he finds them too painful. I asked him if he was all right with my writing them and publishing them. He said, "Yes." He has had no response when something occurred and I said, "Oh, *that's* going in the book." He knows it is not only people at war who pay the price. He has, however, offered many details when I have asked. Thank you for those details and more . . . for offering me the freedom to write this.

I thank the military men and women, the parents, daughters and sisters, sons and brothers, and people who have not experienced the price of combat, but who are writers and as a result friends of mine—Judith Aftergut, Cynthia Akagi, Annette Billings, Kate Boesser, Eileen Clark, Susan Farmer, Duane Herrmann, Beth Hovind, Val Ireland, Fran Kelso, Brenna McLaughlin, Marcia Malott, Laura Morris, Karen Sargent, Theresa Steinlage, Karla Tedtsen, Maria Vega, Kim Warren, and Max Yoho. I also thank my retired military friend, Ray Shultz, who has read some of these writings and offered his support and comments.

Ed and Onecia Mercer, fellow writers, were there for me when Robert was deployed and I was a school principal and chair of the unit's family support group. I remain grateful for their support and continued friendship. I thank Onecia for she is the person I call and say that Robert just said or did such and so. "Yes, Vietnam," or "Yep, Ed does that too." She reassures me that life is normal for this military wife.

Literary magazines and committees offered early encouragement when they published some of these poems and stories and gave me awards for others—the Alaska Poetry Contest, the Alaska State Fair, *Scroll in Space*, *Poetry Repairs*, *Inscape*, and *Reflections*.

I extend my thanks to Marcia Malott for her excellent copyediting. I would also like to thank Dee Horne, editor of *Scroll in Space* literary web journal, and John Horvath, the editor of *Poetry Repairs*, the poetry web journal, for his continued interest in my poetry. Their faith in my work provides its own reward.

I met my publisher, Christopher Robbins, twenty-some years ago when he was the editor for my first two novels. We still keep the friendship and professional relationship we developed then. As founder and president of Familius, I thank him for his continued support of my writing and interest in this book of reflections. I also thank Familius editor, Michele Robbins. She was tireless and put up with my questions and idiosyncrasies with her usual grace and insight.

I am grateful to Donna Lee, wife of Li-Young Lee, for stating her curiosity that started me on the journey of this book, "Tell me about your camel."

Sources

Calkin, Abigail B. 1990. "Changes in Behavior as the Result of the Death of a Relative." *Journal of Precision Teaching* 7: 74–78.

Calkin, Abigail B. October 11, 2001. "WTC & Counting Depressed Behavior." Message posted to SCListServe. http://lists.psu.edu/archives/sclistserv. html.

Dillenburger, K., and M. Keenan. 2001. "Islands of Pain in a Sea of Change: Behaviour Analysis and Bereavement." *European Journal of Behavior Analysis* 2: 187–207.

Enoch, Mark. 1990. "410th to Deploy: 410th Members Answer Call." *Topeka Capital-Journal*, November 22, p. A 1.

About the Author

ABIGAIL B. CALKIN was born in Boston and reared in New England and New York's Greenwich Village. Her first novel, *Nikolin,* was shortlisted for a Benjamin Franklin award and a number of her poems have received awards also. Recently published is *The Night Orion Fell,* a nonfiction book about a commercial fishing accident and Coast Guard rescue. She also has had other poetry, behavior analysis articles, fiction, and nonfiction published. Calkin gives workshops on self-respect and on PTSD. She is writing a second book on commercial fishing and the Coast Guard, and also a sequel to *The Soul of My Soldier,* which will include stories from family members of military men and women. She lives in the Alaskan bush with her husband where they enjoy the landscape and ocean. In addition to writing and consulting, she also gardens, cans, knits, laughs a lot, and enjoys the company of others.

About Familius

Welcome to a place where parents are celebrated, not compared. Where heart is at the center of our families, and family at the center of our homes. Where boo-boos are still kissed, cake beaters are still licked, and mistakes are still okay. Welcome to a place where books—and family— are beautiful. Familius: a book publisher dedicated to helping families be happy.

Visit Our Website: www.familius.com

Our website is a different kind of place. Get inspired, read articles, discover books, watch videos, connect with our family experts, download books and apps and audiobooks, and along the way, discover how values and happy family life go together.

Join Our Family

There are lots of ways to connect with us! Subscribe to our newsletters at www. familius.com to receive uplifting daily inspiration, essays from our Pater Familius, a free ebook every month, and the first word on special discounts and Familius news.

Become an Expert

Familius authors and other established writers interested in helping families be happy are invited to join our family and contribute online content. If you have something important to say on the family, join our expert community by applying at:

www.familius.com/apply-to-become-a-familius-expert

Get Bulk Discounts

If you feel a few friends and family might benefit from what you've read, let us know and we'll be happy to provide you with quantity discounts. Simply email us at specialorders@familius.com.

Website: www.familius.com

Facebook: www.facebook.com/paterfamilius

Twitter: @familiustalk, @paterfamilius1

Pinterest: www.pinterest.com/familius

The most important work

you ever do will be within the

walls of your own home.

CPSIA information can be obtained
at www.ICGtesting.com
Printed in the USA
FSOW02n0342290815
10436FS